The Rise of the Modern Vegan

Printed in the USA
First Printing, 2020
ISBN 978-0-473-50916-3
Published by: White Rockit Books
            Tauranga – New Zealand

White Rockit Books

Liability Disclaimer

The Rise of the Modern Vegan

21st Century Veganism

Fee O'Shea

Dedicated to:

My children, because they have always put up with the whimsical ramblings of their adoring mother.

and

Kathy Wilson who came into my life at just the right moment to spur me on to greater things.

Acknowledgement.

A huge thank you to Caleb Day who patiently helped me navigate through the chapter on religion. Through his knowledge I learned so much and was able to understand the role animals played through the old testament.

Introduction

With the increasing acceptance of veganism, there come some nuances, and this is giving rise to a modern idea about what it means to be a vegan. With the current climate crises, many are seeing animal agriculture as a contributing factor and therefore, are changing to a plant-based diet. Many others are concluding that the standard western diet may not be as healthy as they have been led to believe and are also turning to a plant-based diet. Does this mean they are vegan?

As with my other books, this is an opinion piece backed up by what I have learned, science, trends, and personal research. Our world is changing rapidly, and the environmental impact of climate change is setting us on a path of destruction. It even has its own category – The Sixth Extinction. Nothing new really, global warming has been talked about, discussed, and scientifically researched since the early 19th century.

Here in New Zealand, we got to know about the Ozone layer in the mid-eighties when it was discovered above the Antarctic. CFCs (chlorofluoro-carbons) were blamed and, like the plastics today, there was a global push to get these gases out of circulation. This affected the movers and shakers that sprayed abundance of hairspray over their large styles and every household, on average, had around thirty aerosol cans of something for every different purpose known to man.

By the late 1990s, CFC production (also gases used as coolants in refrigerators) had all but stopped, and all cans are now ozone-safe. It does not mean the ozone layer is fixed, and some scientists say it will be beyond 2050 before we return to how it was pre the CFCs.

In 2019 the ozone hole above New Zealand was the smallest on record. However, that result is caused by warm stratospheric temperatures that put the brakes on ozone loss. Perhaps the warming of the climate overall may benefit the ozone – sadly not the planet.

Several new documentaries, backed by scientific data, were launched, and this made people question their health in regards to what they were eating.

Then there are the animals – the real victims in this ever-changing planet. Both wild and domestic are suffering because of the actions of humans. The environmental movement that caught on in 2019 seems to be the driver for veganism. However, it still remains that true vegans are more concerned about animal welfare.

This book explores what it means to be vegan, answers some of the age-old questions and myths that surround veganism and looks at the myriad of nuances that have risen up with the modern-day plant-based consumer who loosely uses the term 'vegan'.

I'm hoping that you will find the contents of this book interesting enough that, if you are plant-based, vegetarian or omnivore, you will understand more of the ethical side and decide to begin a journey to embracing the true meaning veganism.

If you are thinking about reducing your meat, ditching the dairy, and generally taking control back around what you eat, then there are my easy '7 Steps' near the end that may help point you in the right direction.

And just so you know, half a billion fewer animals were killed in 2018 compared to 2007 simply because more people are eating less meat.

No matter your reason for getting on this trend, be it animals, health, or the planet; all three will be dramatically impacted – that is a fact.

I'll leave you now to get on with the reading.

Note: This book was published at the end of 2019 before the outbreak of the COVID-19 pandemic. 2020 saw a large swing in plant-based foods production as people began to understand the ramifications of animal agriculture. There is no mention of the significant rise in veganism that the virus has caused.

1 – A Trend Begins

2018 heralded in a new trend that quickly took hold and gained momentum as the year progressed, primarily through the UK, the USA and even into Australia and New Zealand.

The trend was veganism.

By the end of the year, Australia topped the list of countries for trend growth also coming in as the third fasted growing market for vegan products according to Euromonitor International. Second on the list was the UK and New Zealand clinched a very respectable third spot. But the surprise was China with a growth rate for vegan products of 17.2 per cent between 2015 and 2020.

Hashtags such as #vegan #ditchdairy #veganuary #govegan #whatveganseat #stopeatinganimals were touted over social media by vegans using them with pride.

One of the best examples which showed the rise in veganism came out at the beginning of 2018 with the hashtag #februdairy. This hashtag had been coined by Dr Jude Capper, who had been the dairy industry's 'Woman of the Year' for 2017. As is an independent Livestock Sustainability Consultant based in the UK, she held quite a bit of sway within the industry.

Let me fill you in on a bit of the back story. In January 2014 a British couple, Jane and Matthew, decided to make January a month of promoting veganism. It started slowly with the hashtag #veganuary, but by 2018 the momentum had grown, and a record 250,000 people across 193 countries had signed up to the challenge of going vegan for a month. What was pleasing to the cause was the number of people who stayed vegan well after the promotional #veganuary had finished.

Hot on the heels of #veganuary 2018 came Dr Jude Capper with the campaign for February 2018 being #februdairy. Dr Capper, encouraged dairy farmers to promote their product by sending positive messages over social media. She began the campaign on Twitter to counter the effects of the roaring success of the #veganuary campaign the month before. The trouble was that it went absolutely pear-shaped when the vegans totally hijacked the hashtag and turned it into a #ditchdairy catchphrase.

Dr Capper had said on twitter

> "Let's make Februdairy happen this year. 28 days, 28 positive dairy posts".

One did wonder if the dairy industry wasn't starting to get a little nervous with the growth of plant milk and the massive response to #veganuary. In actual fact, the #februdairy campaign came as no surprise.

The year before had seen Emily Norton, the co-founder of Norton's Dairy, write a blog in which she said

> "February is the month of Saint Valentine after all, so a little cow love can go a long way for all of us".

The vegans had come back with comments like:

> *"Stop taking the babies away."*
>
> *"Stop artificially inseminating."*
>
> *"Stop killing the male calves."*
>
> *"Stop forcing them into pregnancies."*
>
> *"Stop making them produce more milk."*
>
> *"Stop taxing their bodies so that in five years they are so worn out, no longer financially viable and so they are sent to slaughter and only good for cheap hamburgers or pet food."*
>
> *"If that's a little 'cow love' pfffff we must have read the wrong dictionary on the meaning of the word 'love'."*

From then on, the vegans, who were growing in numbers, kept an eye out for any social media posts regarding animal agriculture so that they could pounce on it and turn it to their advantage.

When Dr Capper tweeted that she wanted 28 days of positive posts, the vegans fired back saying that they'd do 28 days of exposing the real animal practice associated with dairy farming. And they did just that. With every positive dairy post came an outpouring of tweets and comments from the vegan community. It was really quite comical if you took away the powerfully sad message and imagery behind the tweets.

Even at a conference of the National Farming Union in Glasgow, Scotland's president, Andrew McCornick said the initiative wasn't necessarily a good idea.

Going on to say:

"I just feel it adds fuel to the fire, and opens dairy farmers, in particular, to more criticism, and it ends up being counterproductive."

By the time the month finished an analysis of the top hashtags had shown that #govegan and #vegan still reigned supreme, #dairy came in third and #februdairy was relegated much further down the list. But even more significant was that the top 21 twitter accounts for the month belonged to vegans.

The following month the vegans didn't lighten up as #meatlessmarch began. They kept hammering home the point that veganism was on the rise and there was little the animal agriculture industry could do about it.

Billboards started appearing, Vegan YouTubers started getting more traction, Facebook vegan groups increased, and Instagram started to get more vegan foodies and activists. Along with that, people such as James Aspey and Ed Winters (Earthling Ed) started appearing in mainstream media and then the floodgates opened as more and more stars came out to say they had gone vegan, (most for the animals).

The number of documentaries that were being released in 2018 and 2019 was also on the rise from previous years. Movies like 'What The Health' 'Eating Animals' 'The Invisible Vegan' and 'Okja" were followed by 'Eating Our Way To Extinction' 'The Yoyo Effect' ending the year with a feature documentary by award-winning director James Cameron. Even before its release, 'The Game Changers' was set to make waves especially with men's health and those into sports.[1] This documentary shines the light on elite plant-based athletes, soldiers, visionary scientists and cultural icons who all thrive on a vegan diet. The fact that one of the world's strongest men is vegan was an excellent role model for those meat-eaters who cling to the myth that one needs meat for protein.

Once released, this documentary made waves throughout the meat-eating communities with influences like Joe Rogan bringing guests into his podcast who could critically poke holes in the movie and thus appease his followers. It didn't matter how hard the naysayers hit; this was one documentary that advanced the rise of veganism. It was influencers like Kai Greene, a pro-bodybuilder, announcing that he was going plant-based after watching the documentary that inspired his followers to do the same. Twitter had a meltdown, and social media exploded with comments like:

> *"I've been cutting down eating meat a lot recently, and often go days full vegan, but after watching this, I'm completely sold."*

> *"Watched The Game Changers yesterday ... it was a game-changer. Today's viewing is What The health. Bye bye meat!"*

By the time 2018 came to an end, it had appeared that veganism was on the rise much to the chagrin of the meat and dairy industries. Just before the New Year, John Parker, a correspondent for the magazine The Economist, declared in a special edition 'The World in 2019' that it would be the year of the vegan. Millennials had taken

---

[1] now available on Netflix and other networks.

the lead and were fully embracing the vegan eating and business and governments would surely follow.

How right he was. Even early into 2019, it was apparent this was a trend that was not about to go away no matter what the animal industry did. In fact, the more animal agriculture, along with their government bias, tried to defend or promote their products, the more the vegans pushed back through social media, billboards and well-organised activism. It looked like there was going to be one helluva fight with neither side giving in.

In the world of politics, animal agriculture was a huge player. Most countries in the OECD supported their farmers and 'big ag', as it was termed, wielded a lot of power through lobbyists and the money that they poured into the economy. Here in New Zealand dairy stands as the second-highest industry (after tourism) earning the country $7.8 billion to the total GDP. This comprised of dairy farming $5.96 billion and dairy processing $1.88 billion. So, you can see why the New Zealand government didn't want to do anything to upset the balance.

Getting a bit further into 2019, there were murmurings on the New Zealand grapevine that the largest dairy company was looking at ways to incorporate plant-based milk. This would be a significant step in the right direction if they could encourage the farmers to begin to decrease their herd size and start planting crops that could be used for 'milk'. However, by publication nothing had developed so perhaps it was just wishful thinking on the part of the vegans.

When legalisation changed for the growing of hemp late 2018 a whole new industry had arrived. Perhaps this was the future for dairy farmers? Not only is hemp an amazing plant for food, clothing and a variety of other products, but it is also perfect for the soil and the environment, areas that dairy decimates.

With further pressure on the government to do something about reducing emissions for their target to be one hundred per cent carbon neutral by 2050, as well as cleaning up the waterways, the reduction in dairy herds would be a good step in the right direction. How likely that will be is anyone's guess simply because of the money that is being made in dairy farming (as already mentioned).

Most countries, especially the primary producing ones, continued to support animal agriculture as was witnessed in April 2019 in Australia.

A well organised vegan activist protest happened for one day right across Australia. It was a peaceful protest for the animals where activists went onto farms, chained themselves to abattoirs as well as stopping a line of pigs being sent to the gas chambers for slow and frightening suffocation. But the highlight was a sit-in on a busy Melbourne city crossroads where protesters block traffic, including trams, causing traffic to halt at peak time. Finally, the press descended, and there was an absolute out-cry at what the protesters were doing.

So precisely what was the message these activists were trying to give? All they asked was that people watch the Australian documentary 'Dominion' which had been released exactly a year before.

The Prime Minister, Scott Morrison, came out with words like "green criminals" and "anti-Australian" and in a media statement said that the Australian government was prepared to join a legal challenge if any landholder wanted to launch legal action against animal rights activists protesting on their farms.

> "if there are pastoralists, farmers, graziers, that are in a position to bring a civil action against these groups looking to undermine their livelihood, the commonwealth is totally open to supporting them in a test case to show these green criminals it's not on"

The media got behind the government, not surprisingly as the chairman of Channel 7, one of Australia's most prominent media networks, Kerry Stokes, is himself a beef ranching billionaire owning a million hectares of farmland around Australia. But the message they tried to portray was that the vegans were just shooting themselves in the foot and this day of activism would do more harm than good to the cause. How wrong they were. Within 48 hours, over 55 thousand people had viewed 'Dominion' – exactly what the activists had asked for.

Another big coup for the vegan movement was Ed Winters, known as Earthling Ed. being asked to give a lecture at Yale University. The subject being 'Animals as Commodities'. I must admit that I would have loved being a fly on the wall not only to listen but to hear the conversations afterwards as students absorbed the information.

Ed, who hails from Britain, is a great speaker with a very gentle delivery but a message that is totally on point. He has given a couple of TEDx talks that are well worth watching (links in the resource chapter). He not only spoke at Yale, but at other Universities as well such as Brown, Cornell, Columbia, and Rutgers

Another activist who emerged as a leader during this time was Joey Carbstrong. Joey is an Australian with a strong YouTube following who battles with the mainstream media without fear. He brought to light a very biased Channel 7 program that was obviously pro-beef and anti-vegan. Joey had been interviewed for this program and had many of the things he'd said taken entirely out of context.

Not one to 'let it go', Joey delved into what was behind this biased piece of journalism and discovered the chairman Kerry Stokes as mentioned earlier. No wonder he had it in for the vegans! But what it did show once again, was the animal agriculture's fear of the rise of veganism.

Australian vegan activist, James Aspey, shot to fame in 2015 when he appeared on the television morning show Sunrise. How he had got there was a remarkable feat.

James had realised that animals couldn't speak. He later came to the understanding that they did indeed have voices, but no-one heard their screams before they had the throats slit or were gassed. On the first day of January 2014, James decided that, as a way of paying tribute to these voiceless animals, he would take a vow of silence for one year. During this time, he travelled across Australia trying to get the message to others with the intention to:

> *"inspire others to live in alignment with what they already believe (that animals deserve to be free from unnecessary suffering and death) by adopting a vegan ethic."*

As the year drew to a close, he was asked to go on a national television show and speak his first words there. What an opportunity. So, on the morning of 13th January 2015, James sat with the breakfast hosts. When Andrew O'Keefe asked him why he did this, James looked directly into the camera, broke his silence and said:

> *"Thank you for asking.*
> *The reason I took a vow of silence was to raise awareness for the voiceless victims of this planet - the animals. We all say we love animals, and we all are against animal cruelty, but we pay people to mutilate, torture and slaughter animals. And it's not for any necessity. It's not because we need to for our health. It's just because we like the way they taste. So, I went voiceless because they're voiceless. They cry in pain, they scream in terror, and when they do that, they're using their voice to tell us they're suffering. I did it to raise awareness for them."*

From that moment on, James became someone to follow. He is known for his consistently calm and friendly speaking manner when debating non-vegans, and to this day he travels the world speaking to those who will listen about veganism, all of which he does voluntarily. In 2019, Aspey was a candidate for the Animal Justice Party in the New South Wales state election. Although he wasn't successful this time, in 2015 the party won its first seat in the New South Wales Legislative Council then in 2019 they won a second seat. In 2018 the AJP won its first seat in the Victorian Legislative Council.

Getting animal rights activists into government roles was a massive win for the vegan movement.

There doesn't seem to be one particular event that began this trend. More like a grass-roots movement by passionate and committed people whose only thought is the plight of the billions of land animals bred into existence and killed every year. Add the wild and farmed fish, and we're looking at around three billion killed <u>every day</u> for food.

Around the world, the percentage of vegans and plant-based eaters rises each year. In the USA alone only one per cent of consumers were vegan in 2014, but by 2017 that number had increased to six per cent. Searching Google Trends showed an impressive increase worldwide with the top countries, including Israel, Australia, Canada, Austria and New Zealand. More and more people are using the word 'vegan' as a search term to find recipes, products, stores, documentaries, and general information. By mid-2019 the movement was definitely on an upward trajectory.

Even China, whose citizens use meat as a means of status, has released new dietary guidelines encouraging their people to reduce their meat consumption by fifty per cent, and it is predicted that China's vegan market will grow more than seventeen per cent by 2020.

As more influencers, celebrities and athletes adopt veganism growth will rise exponentially. According to researchers from the University of Pennsylvania and the University of London, it takes around 25 per cent of the population to push a belief from the fringes into the mainstream.
Now here's a bit of maths for you or maybe it's just my daft logic. Let me use the figures just mention before.

In 2014 research by GlobalData in the USA found that one per cent of people were vegan. (Now I'm thinking that quite possibly the number could have been higher as back then it wasn't really the done thing to be aligning yourself to veganism if you wanted to appear 'normal'). By 2017 the number had risen to six per cent.

By my calculation, and I'm certainly not the best mathematician in the world, so I do stand corrected – that makes a growth of, say, five per cent per year. Which would mean the USA will reach the magic 25 per cent before 2030. That certainly is a bright future for the animals, planet and mankind.

With big organisations and corporations jumping on the vegan bandwagon, this growth is not a fad. It is the way of the future. Because of the massive interest from large organisations the meat and dairy industries were really getting the wind up. In 2017 the EU Court of Justice confirmed a ban on products which were purely plant-based using the terms 'milk', 'cream', 'butter', 'cheese' or 'yoghurt' as a marketing tool. These terms were to be used only for products of animal origin. But this is where it becomes a bit of a travesty, because exempt is coconut milk, nut butter and ice cream. The dairy industry seems to think that the consumer is not very intelligent at all and would not be able to distinguish the word 'almond' from 'cow'. In Canada laws also exist that prohibit dairy alternatives being labelled as milk, protecting the word as meaning 'the lacteal secretion obtained from the mammary gland of a cow'. With that I'm thinking don't they mean 'animal' because where does it leave the goat? And in the USA, there is bipartisan support for the Dairy Pride Act, this would direct the FDA to give a clear definition of milk. The Australian government is currently trying to push for the same ban.

With all the hoo-ha on words, it was rather apparent that the dairy industry was running scared. My personal view is that the quibbling over semantics is not going to stop the eventual demise of dairy as we know it today.

But it's not only dairy. The EU was pushing for words like 'sausage' 'burger' 'steak' to be only associated with animal parts and not to be used on plant-based products. In mid 2019 the vegan and vegetarian campaigners opposed the proposal arguing that terms such as 'veggie burger' and veggie sausage' have been used for decades and questioned the reason for the drive to restrict such phrasing. There had never been a complaint laid that a consumer had been misled.

> "It's obviously an attempt to attack vegetarian meat substitutes. For me, it's number one a sign that the meat lobby is worried about a rapid change in diets, especially among young people – a lot of which is about their response to climate change,"
> -   Green MEP Molly Scott Cato

The silly part is that the words' milk' 'meat' 'cheese' 'sausage' etc. tell a consumer what a product can be used for, not what's in it. For example, you can get a beef and pork sausage or you can get a veggie sausage. Both can be used to grill on the BBQ – one has beef and pork in it and the other has vegetables. I don't see what the problem is other than animal ag running scared.

And while on the subject of specific words. In mid-2019, the New South Wales Farmers, (Australia), at their annual conference decided to change the terminology for the livestock industry. They agreed that the word 'slaughter' had negative connotations and opted to change it to 'process'.

It came up because the members realised that if the word 'slaughter' was Googled it would give the wrong idea.

> "The word slaughter is not appropriate for our industry as we are processing animals through the various stages that end up for food. It's not a mass murder."
> -   Mr Jack Skipper

Of course, that is a debatable statement as the number of animals killed in any single day accounts for the word 'mass'. And perhaps the fact both the animal instinctively does not want to die, and the killing is deliberate - could that equate to 'murder'?

In May 2018 the vegan charity Viva! Began a month-long campaign urging the public to ditch dairy. Titled 'MooFree May' it encouraged people to swap the dairy products they use for the plant-based versions. This was to educate them how their health, animal welfare and the environment all suffer because of dairy.

It was run predominantly through social media; however, there were also organised outreach events in major cities across the UK. It was a great time to be handing out free vegan cheeses and chocolates for the public to taste. Along with the free tastings were the videos showing undercover footage taken on dairy farms. However, the campaign also presented a strong nutritional case for going dairy-free as well as pointing out the environmental impact dairy farming has. An ongoing event #moofreemay was out in force again the following year to even more significant success.

Of course, May has also been classed as #meatfreemay and many companies as well as organisations use this month to promote their meat-free products. Other plant-based organisations also use it to push the vegan challenges with meal plans, guides, and support.

Eating vegan is one of those things that does need a bit of guidance if one is going to be healthy at the same time.

My personal suggestion is "if you're going vegan, then why not do it the healthiest way possible?" Mind you, there is a rather big leap from eating meals that are animal-based to whole plant foods, but it's definitely worth it for your health. If you think of it as not 'what' you are giving up, but what you are gaining with all the new foods, then the process is so much easier.

June 2019 marked the second yearly 'Summer Vegan Pledge' organised by Animal Aid, one of the UK's largest animal rights organisations. Many trendy and well-known UK vegan restaurants offered discounts to those who took the 30-day pledge in order to support the movement.

The success of Veganuary, Summer Vegan Pledge, Moofreemay, as well as countless other numbered day pledges, is now well documented. Each year sees a remarkable growth in the number of people trying vegan, and those who stay plant-based is far greater than those who fall off and revert back.

The majority who do revert back will limit the amount of animal products they consume simply because they have felt the benefits of the plant-based diet and know about the animal suffering. These people and those who support other vegans such as parents with vegan children are known as Vegan Allies[2] and should have the vegan's respect as, in their way, they are getting the message out there and supporting the cause.

At the end of 2019, a 76-page report was put out by ReThinkX[3] titled 'The Second Domestication of Plants and Animals, the Disruption of the Cow, and the Collapse of Industrial Livestock Farming.'
The report was eye-opening, stating that the US cattle industry will effectively be bankrupt before 2030 also affecting those farmers who grow food specifically for these animals. It also predicted that other livestock industries such as pigs, chicken and fish would follow close behind.

If RethinkX is right, this will mean a drastic change in how the land is used. Currently, 80% of the agricultural land is designated to farmed animals and their feed. A substantial amount will be free to grow plant proteins as well as being put back into much needed natural ecosystems. Not only will it be better for the environment, but the use of water will be much more efficient, and there will be significantly less waste.

As demand declines for animal products, governments will have to remove the subsidies that are currently propping up these industries. It was interesting to see that, in January 2019, Canada removed dairy from its healthy food pyramid. However, in the following August budget the government announced a package of nearly four billion to

[2] Term coined by Dr Melanie Joy
[3] an independent think tank that analyses and forecasts the speed and scale of technology-driven disruption and its implications across society. Produces impartial, data-driven analyses that identify pivotal choices to be made by investors, business, policy and civic leaders.

aid the dairy, poultry and egg industries as a type of compensation for European trade deals that were a huge hit to them. Dairy in Canada will be affected at home with the removal from the food pyramid, and this could be the beginning of the end for them, especially if there are no more hand-outs.

In 2019 oral testimony began in the US for the 2020 Dietary Guidelines Advisory Committee. Individual doctors, along with the Physicians Committee for Responsible Medicine[4] testified that dairy should be removed. If this happens, there will be a significant shift away from dairy, and we may, in fact, see its demise.

The increase in technologies such as cellular agriculture and precision fermentation will go a long way to satisfying the meat-eating market, and, as they become less expensive, the fast-food industry will ultimately use this type of 'meat' in their products. There's no doubt that animals for food will still exist. However, they will be, as in the past, for kings and poachers and the rest of the riff-raff will have to make do with the plant alternatives. If this is the case, it will be interesting to see what the health of the average person will be.

I'm going to end this chapter back on Twitter and the hilarious tweets and comments that flew around from British show host Piers Morgan, a man who is vehemently anti-vegan and who takes great delight in slamming the movement and the food whenever he can.

The most publicised row happened when chef Gordon Ramsay, also renowned for being anti-vegan to the point he had publicly said he'd

---

[4] a non-profit with over 12,000 doctor members

pay his children not to be vegetarian, introduced a vegan Sunday roast to his London restaurant. Ramsay tweeted:

> *"It's happened ... the #vegan roast has landed @breadstkitchen ! #roastrevolution"*

It was sacrilege according to Piers who tweeted back:

> *"Oh FFS, Ramsay ... not you as well? This looks utterly revolting. (sick emojis)"*

Piers Morgan had taken a shot at Greggs when they launched their vegan sausage roll (which, I'll add has been such a success they are bringing out more vegan choices).
On launch, Greggs tweeted:

> *"The wait is over ... 3.1.19 #vegansausageroll (emoji plant happy face)."*

Morgan tweeted response:

> *"Nobody was waiting for a vegan bloody sausage, you PC-ravaged clowns."*

Greggs came straight back with:

> *"Oh hello Piers, we've been expecting you."*

Morgan appeared on Goodmorning Britain to taste the vegan sausage roll. He declared it to "stink", and on tasting it, spat it out into a trashcan. However, the other two hosts also tried it and said it was delicious.

From then on, all the comments and tweets that Piers did became rather a joke and, instead of diminishing sales of vegan foods, producers got on board with the 'negative advertising' he was doing and turned it around to their advantage.

And Chef Ramsay? He believes that Morgan should get with the times, even going so far as to advise other chefs to embrace the vegan revolution as it's here to stay.

With all that said. What does it actually mean to be vegan? Let's truck on over to the next chapter and find out.

2 – What it Means to be Vegan

Before I start talking about what it means to be vegan, I thought it would be a good idea to give you all the different varieties of names attributed to people based on what they eat. This type of classification has become quite the thing over the last few years, and more categories seem to be added to the list as more people identify with a specific food group.

So, here we go:

Carnivore - Only eats meat, reserved more for the animal kingdom although I'm sure there are people out there who don't like veggies and would be more carnivore than anything else!

Herbivore – Usually restricted to the plant-eaters of the animal kingdom, but in fact, is what humans are, as I will explain in the health chapter.

Omnivore - These people eat everything - red meat, white meat, fish, vegetables, MacD's, KFC, etc. However, they are generally meat-eaters with animal products eaten at every meal. (Includes dairy and eggs). So, predominantly meat with some plants on the plate.

Flexitarian – This person eats plant-based meals interspersed with meat. They are predominantly plant-based eaters with the odd bit of meat thrown in for good measure - in other words a picky omnivore! As the plant-based movement grows more and more people are becoming flexitarian. This has the emphasis of predominately plants on their plate as well as having meatless days. This is usually a precursor to vegetarian and then to vegan, a lovely journey and one that benefits both the animals and the planet.

Pescetarian - A person whose meat choice is fish. I found a couple of other names for this classification on the net Vegaquarians or Fish-and-Chip-ocrits, which I thought was delightful.

Pollo-vegetarian - Eats no red meat or fish, but does eat poultry.

Pollo-pescetarian - Add poultry to the fish, and you have a pollo-pescetarian. For me, this is just an omnivore! People who eat this way usually say they don't eat red meat.

Lacto-vegetarian – Eats no meat, poultry, seafood or eggs but does consume dairy products (usually cheese).

Ovo-vegetarian - Eats no meat, poultry, seafood or dairy products but does eat eggs.

Lacto-ovo-vegetarian – These people don't eat meat, poultry, or seafood, but do eat both eggs and dairy products. This is probably the most common vegetarian as both eggs and dairy are currently considered to come within the definition of a vegetarian.

100 per cent Vegetarian – Only eats plants but does wear or use animals' products in other ways.

Entovegan - a person who eats insects. Entomophagy is the practice of eating insects that includes their eggs, larvae, pupae and adults.

So batting at mosquitoes and midges, some vegans won't even do that, but others believe that it is self-defence as many mosquitoes do carry diseases such as malaria.

However, there's a big difference from batting a free-flying mosquito to actually cultivating and harvesting insects to eat. Most vegans do not accept someone who eats insects to be vegan.

Vegan - Does not eat anything that comes from an animal either land or sea, nor uses any animal products. However, it does go way beyond this, which I will get into further on.

Wholefood plant-based – A completely 100 per cent vegetarian diet but the emphasis is on the healthy attributes of the food. All food is whole, in other words, not processed wherever possible. Example: olives are whole food, but olive oil is processed.

Raw/living foodists – 100 per cent vegetarian, these people eat at least 75 per cent uncooked (items may be heated up to 48°C 118°F), unprocessed, organic fruits and vegetables, to preserve more vitamins and minerals. The pure raw foodists are slowly growing. Many people (especially vegans) 'eat raw' at least occasionally. It is recommended to have some raw foods each day even if it is only in the form of salads, nuts and fruits. Raw foods are very nutritious.

Fruitarians - Eats fruit and seeds only.

Other names that all pretty much mean the same:

Vegavores - Someone who very rarely eats meat ... perhaps once a month. Used more with the Paleo way of eating.

  Carnesparian – Mostly vegetarian with sporadic meat-eating.

Reducetarian – The latest word I've come across, meaning those who are trying to reduce the amount of animal products they consume.

As you can see, there are all sorts of varieties of food groups, but there are also two central **Belief Systems** that determine the way people view animals.

Carnism – this is an invisible belief system that conditions people to eat and use certain animals and not others. It is currently the predominant belief system in the Western world. It is what switches off a person's empathy to any suffering of any animal that is deemed to be needed for the sole purpose of food, advancing or entertaining humanity.

Veganism – this is the complete opposite. It is a belief that all animals, (including sea life), are sentient beings and should not be used for any purpose be that food, clothing, experiments, entertainment or work - veganism switches on empathy.
Unless you are born into a vegan family, you inherently and unconsciously adopt carnism as the belief, that is why it is 'invisible'. The veganism belief system is learned later on in life through the thought process.

Before I move on, there are a couple more words that go along with veganism (although not used very often), they do fit in with modern thinking. They are Sufficientarianism and Compassionism. Let me explain.

Sufficientarians are people who are perhaps a bit more pragmatic and believe in distributive justice. In other words, rather than being concerned with inequalities, they aim at making sure each of us has enough. Their aim regarding the ethics of avoiding animal products is not to be absolutely vegan, or maximally vegan, but to be sufficiently vegan. This means making as much effort that is feasible to reduce harm to animals for the sake of diet.

Compassionism. Obviously, this comes from the word compassion and is another way of explaining veganism. As the term veganism may offend people, some vegans will use this word instead to describe their lifestyle.

I'll slip another word in here that is also more diet-related, and that is **Vegantarian**. People adopting this style will probably also avoid Californian avocados, which use bees that have to be trucked in from thousands of miles away. Some say this is animal abuse as the bees have to be enclosed in their hives for the journey.

True vegans choose veganism. The basis of this is, of course, the animals. It is ethically and morally based, naturally embraces all the plant-based foods, vegan clothing, medicines, entertainment and any other area that uses animals. What is important is the animals, not the food. Vegans coming from this angle are more likely to be outspoken, participate in some form of activism and promote veganism when and wherever possible.

When a person decides to delve a little deeper into the vegan phenomena, it's like opening Pandora's box. It's like the old saying "once you've learnt something, there's no going back", and this holds true especially when you open your eyes and see the cruelty and abuse that is shown to animals. Once seen – you can't 'unsee'. It is why many choose the veganism lifestyle after watching a documentary like Earthlings or Dominion. If you have any fibre of empathy in your body at all, you just cannot justify eating animal flesh or drinking animal mammary fluids, (breast milk).

How the phenomena actually started is a bit blurred, but one thing is sure, social media has contributed to its growth at an exponential rate. As athletes, actors and other celebrities change to eating plant-based or going vegan so are their fans following suit, or are at least looking into it.

Corporations are picking up on the trend and, at the time of writing, it seems that a new product comes onto the market each week. The 'big boys' of the fast-food industry are also coming out to play by trialling vegan burgers and vegan chicken and getting great success.

One has to understand that the vegan community will happily share any new vegan product through social media. The vegans will support the item to help the cause.

A brilliant example of this was the launch of the vegan Magnums by Unilever. The vegans flocked to buy this 'iced confection' so much so that many places couldn't keep up with the demand. Needless to say, Unilever has now made this a standard item.

Being vegan is a 'way of life'. It incorporates a lot more than just the food. When you read and understand the definition of veganism;

> 'it is a way of living that excludes, as far as possible and practicable, all forms of exploitation of, and cruelty to, animals for food, clothing or any other purpose'

you realise it has nothing to do with the food and everything to do with the animals and it makes sense that it is a lifestyle.

Once you have fully taken on board the vegan eating and the lifestyle, then you can say you're vegan. If, however, you are just 'eating vegan' and are happy to support other animal activities, e.g. clothing, rodeo, or other animal uses, then you should use the term 'plant-based' or 100 per cent vegetarian.

What is good news is that society seems to have embraced plant-based foods, although perhaps not quite the true meaning of veganism. Still, by accepting and embracing all the different subtleties more people are beginning to adopt and sustain a vegan lifestyle or close to it.

As I mentioned before about how 25 per cent of the population can take an idea from the fringes to the mainstream, I would like to elaborate a bit.

When just 10 per cent of the population adheres to an unshakable belief, that belief will be adopted by the majority. It is achieved by those wanting the change convincing more and more people to question their personal beliefs. As they question and see the reasoning of the new belief, they make the change. Once the number goes above the ten per cent, the new belief system travels like wildfire through the society.

Veganism currently stands at around six per cent overall throughout the first world population. There are signs it will reach the magic ten per cent in a matter of a couple of years which should mean that the 25 per cent mainstream belief will be here by 2030 (purely my own opinion).

3 – Looking at Life Through the Animals' Eyes

I've heard some funny things over the years but this statement;

> *"If animals are not meant to be eaten, then why are they made of meat?"*

has to top them all.

So let's take this opportunity to talk about the animals.

The problem is that we have two kinds of domestic animals –
1. The pet
2. The food.
and both live extraordinarily different lives.

Earlier on, I gave you the reason why people can switch off and on their empathy towards these two categories of animals through the carnistic belief system.

Sadly, there is absolutely no difference between the animal that is bred for being your pet and the animal that is bred for being your food.

And the only thing that makes us different from other animals is that we have developed a complex language. Everything else is similar. Dogs, cats, cows, pigs and all other animals, including us, clearly show affection to one another. All animals have cognitive ability (means the ability to problem solved), and this skill is shown right across the animal world even down to insects.

Zoologists know that some animals have memory and others recognise themselves, so have self-awareness.

All animals show happiness, as well as fear, and all have the absolute desire to live. We also know that animals have pain receptors – if an animal is being hurt, it feels exactly what you would feel if it was you.

One other thing that sets humans apart from other animals is that we are the most violent and deliberately cruel animal of all both within our own species and to others. It appears that all animals will fight over territories, including humans. Yes, some animals are violent. Typically, it is used for survival and not for simple convenience or pleasure. There are always exceptions. The chimpanzee can be quite a violent ape. However, its violence is displayed nowhere near as often as it does in the human species.

These animals are living, breathing, feeling sentient beings that, just like you, want to live their lives the way that nature intended them to.

With your pet, I'm sure you would not:

- Allow it to live in a confined space where it could not turn around.
- Castrate it without anaesthetic.
- Remove its tail without anaesthetic.
- Confine it to a cage so its kittens or puppies could not be looked after properly.
- Grind up its live babies because they are of no use.
- Take infants away from the mother before weaning.
- Allow it to live in its own faeces.

- Leave it out in the hot sun without shade or water.
- Cut off part of its lips without anaesthetic.
- Pull out its claws without anaesthetic.
- Pull out its perfectly good teeth without anaesthetic.

And, I'm sure that when the time came you certainly would not truck it off to get slaughtered, instead you would gently take it to the vet so it could be euthanized under loving care.

Now, as mentioned above, humans can be cruel, and so there are some who would not be so kind to their pet. But I'm talking to you, and I know you have a really gentle heart and your pet is loved so much.

So, what happens in the slaughterhouse?

> *"If slaughterhouses had glass walls, we would not eat meat."*
> *- Sir Paul McCartney*

Animals become frantic as they watch the animal before them in the killing-line being prodded, beaten, electrocuted, and knifed.

There are many, many times that the animal is not even dead before it reaches the skinning or de-feathering part.

There are many animals that try to get back into the truck as they can smell the death and are well aware of what is going to happen to them. But doing this only makes the humans more violent towards them, and consequently, they are prodded with electric prods … think 'taser' – the difference is, this animal is not a criminal.

But it starts way before the animals get to the abattoirs.

The intensive production of animals has created a 'factory' type farming system for your pork, chicken and beef. We can also add dairy cows under that 'beef'" heading as dairy cows are also intensely farmed with little or no regard for the welfare of the animal.

Beef Cattle

The calf stays with its mother until around six to eight months of age. Bull calves are castrated with no anaesthetic and kept. Once weaned, they are left to graze until they reach the desired weight usually around a year old. Depending on the country, the Beef cattle typically spend that first year on the farm grazing the grass just as you see in the marketing pictures. After that they are trucked off to feedlots to be 'finished off', in other words, to get fattened up ready for market.

These feedlots are nothing more than outdoor factory farms. The cattle are put into penned areas with no grass. They usually start out being fed forage, something like alfalfa or wheat hay, then as the animals increase their intake, they transition onto a high energy density diet of grain, soy, and/or corn most often laced with antibiotics and other supplements.

Different countries have different procedures. Some feedlots will vaccinate the cattle on arrival, and some will use the method of a hormone implant to promote feed efficiency.

The cattle will remain on the feedlot for around three to four months, and once they have reached the desired weight as mentioned above, they are taken to be slaughtered and cut into 'prime beef' for your BBQ steaks, prime ribs, brisket and corned beef.

Female calves are typically kept, and once they reach sexual maturity, at around 15 months they are then artificially inseminated delivering their calf nine months later. Female cows (heifers) are re-bred every 12 months. They continue until they are no longer able to breed, (around seven to nine years), then slaughtered and used for either the cheap fast-food burgers or meat for pet food.

Dairy Cows

Male or Bobby calves from the dairy industry have an extremely short life. These calves are taken from their mothers within a few hours from birth. And as there is no money to be made, many are killed on the farm or sent to slaughter. They are killed in different ways, by a bullet, by stun gun, having their throat slit or just brutally hammered to death with a blunt object. The last method is illegal here in New Zealand. However, it is still done and definitely is practiced in other parts of the world where animal welfare is not as strict.

Most farmers will send them off to be slaughtered anywhere between four and ten days old. As a child, I can remember driving past farm gates and seeing these babies crated together waiting for the truck to pick them up. Many times, they were in the hot sun with no water. Now it's very rare to see them at the farm gate due to public pressure, so the trucks go onto the farms to pick them up. There are rules around the handling of these calves, but one law does sadden me. These babies, legally, can go up to 24 hours without food and can spend up to 12 hours on the transport truck, which equates to 12 hours without water either.

Each country will have its own rules on Bobby calves; however, worldwide they are not worth very much to the farmer as they are not beef cattle. Some are used for leather, some are sent to other farms for fattening up for veal, but most are processed into cheap burgers or for pet food. These babies are an extremely sad by-product of the dairy industry.

There is provision made in the law that permits induction at the end of the pregnancy. This is done to keep the cows in sync for the milking program. There is, however, a restriction on the number of inductions that can take place in any one season preventing farmers from bringing all cows into labour at the same time. Not all calves survive the induction.

When the calves are taken the mother cows can be heard bellowing out wildly trying to find their babies. They can be seen running after the cattle trucks that take their calves to a separate part of the farm if female, abattoirs or death if male. I have personally heard these bellows go on for three days and nights, a sound I will never forget.

So, the female calf gets to stay on the farm to help to replenish the herd. She is taken from her mother at birth (like the boys) and put in a separate barn to be fed powdered milk from bottles while her mother is sent back into the milking shed for humans to drink her milk.

Once the young calf is around 18 months old, she will be artificially inseminated. Most farms use this method for a couple of reasons – it keeps the calving timing close together and with herd sizes ever increasing, it is a much more precise practice with a better hit rate than with a bull. Of course, semen has to be collected from bulls, and that's a whole other story of animal abuse.

It's important to note here that during the time the cow is milked, she is pregnant and therefore producing a more considerable amount of hormones which is transferred into the milk. Naturally, the cow must be lactating in order to produce milk. Lactation is the result of giving birth. So, the milking cycle begins once the calf is born.

The cow is around 13 months old when she is first artificially inseminated, and after the birth of her first calf, she immediately goes onto the milking machine. Within three months of delivery, she is inseminated again and goes through about seven months of her nine-month pregnancy still on the milking machine. She is then given a two-month 'dry' period before the birth to allow her udder tissue to regenerate. Immediately after the calf is born the whole cycle begins again.

A cow's natural life span can be up around twenty years; however, a dairy cow's body is so punished and under constant stress with continual pregnancies and continuous milking that her life span ends, on average at around five to seven years old. You have to also take into account that the milk yield (as a result of selective breeding and genetic manipulation) is usually 30-50 litres (8-13 gallons) per day about ten times more than her calf would drink.

Tail docking is another horrific practice. Thankfully it has now been banned in New Zealand however it still goes on in other countries. Docking is done by a hot iron crushing the tail or tying a rubber band around it to stop the blood flow, so it eventually falls off.

Disbudding is another procedure done to remove the buds of horns from the cows. Local anaesthetic should be used, and good farmers will; however, many don't. It can be done with a hot iron or by chemical cauterisation.

Some statistics:

- Dairy cows have, over the years, been genetically bred to increase their milk yield, which is up by around 18 per cent from 10 years ago.
- There are over 264 million dairy cows worldwide.
- Global milk production is around 600 million tonnes every year.
- The largest producer of milk is the USA producing over 87 million tonnes per annum.
- India has the greatest number of dairy cows in the world with over 40 million cows.

Sadly, these beautiful creatures are just milk machines. When a dairy cow and calf is taken to a farm sanctuary, the amount of milk produced diminishes to just enough to feed her calf, and once the calf is weaned the milk flow stops. In these sanctuaries, cows are not forced into pregnancies and usually never put with bulls.

Pigs

Most pigs live in factory farms. These are not natural conditions, and consequently, the pig is unable to perform many of its inherent instincts.

Female pigs are artificially inseminated at around five or six months of age. The pregnancy lasts for three months, three weeks and three days. This means that most sows will be able to produce a litter of around ten to thirteen piglets twice a year.

With this in mind, sows will have between four and seven litters before they become exhausted. It is then that they are slaughtered, like the dairy cow their meat is of little value and therefore used for processed meat such as sausages and other low-quality products.

The natural life span of a pig is between ten and fifteen years; however, farmed pigs only get to around three to five years of age.

So, what happens to the female once she is old enough to be bred? In many countries, she is confined in a sow stall or crate pretty much all of her life only shifting to a farrowing crate to give birth and feed her young. The piglets are weaned at about three weeks and taken from their mother and put into the 'nursery'. That's right, it's called a nursery, but it provides no chance to express natural behaviours such as digging. This is where the young babies are fattened up ready for slaughter.

New Zealand has now banned the use of sow stalls, although they can still be used for a few weeks at the start of pregnancy.
Both sow and farrowing crates give very little room for the sow. She is unable to turn around, and some sow crates are so tight she is even unable to lie down.

The natural instinct of the mother is to prepare a nest to birth her babies in, but sows are supplied no bedding and are often seen biting the bars of the stall or swaying repetitively[5]. Just before she is due to give birth, she is taken from one part of the shed to another

---

[5] Not all countries have the pigs confined during all the pregnancy, however, they usually are confined for insemination and for a couple of months after.

and led into the farrowing crate. This is the only time she is free to walk. Here she can at least lie down but is still unable to turn around. After birth, the mother can do nothing to look after her babies other than lie down to feed them.

At a few days old, male piglets are castrated with no anaesthetic. Tail docking (again without anaesthetic) is routine to prevent the pigs from biting each other's tails in frustration.

Pigs can live up to twelve years; however, they are sent to slaughter when they have reached the desired weight of around 127 kilos - 280 pounds, anywhere between four to seven months old, (younger for bacon). This young age of slaughter is due to selective breeding and, in some cases, weight gaining drugs, the piglets are forced to grow at an alarming rate in order to fatten them up. They are typically fed a diet of corn and soybean meal laced with vitamins and minerals.

In the USA more than eighty per cent of pigs have pneumonia when slaughtered. This is due to the dangerous gases from manure, including the high levels of ammonia that they live in.

Transportation, especially in the USA, can be horrific for these young piglets. They are crammed into huge trucks, quite often not given any food or water for the entire journey, which may be hundreds of miles. They suffer from the diesel fumes and ammonia from urine as well as temperature extremes.

We are slightly better in New Zealand, but not by much. Pigs, just like the Bobby calves, can be on the transport truck for up to 12 hours, that's a long time to go without food or water, especially if you're just a baby!

New Zealanders have also been petitioning the government to get pigs out of the farrowing crates. Since the pigs are no longer in sow stalls, it has meant that farmers have to make more room available and if the ban on farrowing crates happens, that will mean even more room will be needed. The ban will, no doubt, bring down the number of pigs a farmer will be able to have reducing the local supply. Because of this, we have started to increase the volume of pork products we import from China, where the welfare of pigs is pretty much non-existent.

Some piggy facts:

- 1.5 billion pigs are slaughtered worldwide per year.
- Piglets are transferred to pens at three weeks of age to be fattened up for slaughter.
- They are routinely fed antibiotics because diseases spread quickly in the tightly packed conditions.

In 2018 38,000 pigs were slaughtered in China due to African swine fever. By 2019 the swine fever had taken hold and upwards of 200 million pigs were facing the same fate. The rampaging fever named 'pig Ebola' was due in part to poor, overcrowding conditions and at time of writing, is a seriously contagious disease spreading across Asia as well as eastern and central Europe.

Pigs contracting ASF suffer dreadfully from internally haemorrhaging until they die. It currently is not affecting humans; however, there is a chance that it may mutate and pose a risk. The virus can last for several weeks and can travel long distances on people's clothes, on vehicles, and equipment making the spread even more dangerous. It spreads through contact with live or dead pigs as well as via contaminated pork products.

Dirk Pfeiffer, a veterinary epidemiologist at City University of Hong Kong and ASF expert says:

> *"This is the biggest animal disease outbreak we've ever had on the planet. It makes the foot and mouth disease and BSE outbreaks pale in comparison to the damage that is being done. And we have no way to stop it from spreading."*

Scientists have been warning about the health risks that surround such intensive farming. Pigs are kept in filthy, overcrowded conditions which, in China, can be in some 'farm sheds' that are up to seven stories high. They are denied fresh air, space and sunlight, so it's no wonder that disease can quickly spread. These multi-floored farms are becoming more popular. In 2019 construction was already underway for two 13-story factories which include everything from birth to slaughter to process. Each level is a separate 'farm' with its own farm workers. Neither the animals nor the workers will go on any other level until the time of slaughter. Supposedly this is to stop any spread of disease.

This particular company has also invested heavily in AI (artificial intelligence). In late 2019 it unveiled its high-tech artificial intelligence system called FPF (future pig farm/factory) which it is installing into these 'hog hotels' as they have called these high-rise buildings. FPF uses facial and sound recognition, robot assistant, cameras, sensors and other fancy gadgets. It is a 24-hour system that can analyse even each pig's voice, can combine data such as body temperature and how the pig has eaten – a robotic veterinarian. Early warnings mean that action can be taken to avoid any illness.

Now an animal's ID and information gathering on that animal is not new. Dairy farmers have been doing it for years with tags sending data to the farmer's computer giving information concerning milk production and the health of the cow. But the technology in these pig farms goes way beyond this. The idea is to have as little human contact as possible to try and reduce the risk of spreading disease.

Before we leave the technology, another invention has dairy cows in Russia fitted with virtual reality goggles giving the cow the idea that they are in a sun-drenched, green grassy paddock. Supposedly this will relax them and consequently boost milk production. They fail to understand that the cow will not feel the warmth of the sun nor taste the fresh grass.

Pork production, chicken meat and eggs are the most intensive farming practices and are deplorable, unhealthy for both animals and humans and need to be stopped.

Next, let's explore the chicken industry.

Chickens

Meat chickens are known as broilers and are raised in sheds containing as many as 45,000 birds. They grow unnaturally fast due to selective breeding and antibiotics pumped into their food. Chickens have a natural lifespan of 10-15 years, but broilers are slaughtered when they reach six to seven <u>weeks</u> of age.

So, let's go through the process of how you get your roasted chicken, chicken drumsticks or KFC nuggets etc.

Barn sizes do vary, but barns around 155.5 meters - 510 feet long and 13 meters - 43 feet wide can house approximately 34,000 birds at one time. They are hatchlings on day one but grow to full size and weight within the six or seven weeks mentioned above.

The last couple of weeks are very stressful for the birds. By now, they are extremely top-heavy, and many find it difficult to hold their weight on their weak legs. If their legs break, which often happens, the bird can't get to the water or food and so will perish. Depending on when they die, quite often their bodies are left where they fall until harvest time. Another reason they prematurely die is heart failure as, like the legs, the heart is unable to keep up with the excessive weight. Living in such cramped conditions also means they live in their own waste and have to breathe in high levels of ammonia, which irritates their eyes, throats and skin.

At the end of the six to seven weeks, the birds are harvested. All birds are removed from the shed with the live ones being sent off to slaughter. The sheds are then cleaned out, and the whole process starts again with the introduction of the next batch of hatchlings.

At slaughter, the live chicken is flipped upside down by holding onto the legs. It is then tied up. At this point, there is quite a high possibility that the chicken's leg is broken or it's not tied up correctly. The reason the chicken is tied upside down is that they don't have a diaphragm they have air sacs and they breathe by changes in the pressure in these sacs. By being tipped upside down, they can't breathe properly, and so they go into a state of 'calm'.

The live chicken is hooked onto a processing line. The first part of this is to stun the chicken before the killing. The conveyor passes the chicken through water, which has an electric current running through it.
The next process in this automated chain of events is the actual killing, which, in New Zealand, is done by slitting the throat so the chicken will bleed to death. The dead chicken is then put into scalding water for plucking.

If the chicken is not correctly trussed at the beginning, (remember I said that there was a high possibility that this might happen), it can miss being dunked into the water. A bird that is not stunned at the start can begin to twist around, and therefore the killing blade can miss the throat. The outcome is that the chicken will be put into the boiling water still alive.

Wait a minute - don't we already do that with crayfish and lobster?

Chickens Raised for Eggs

In egg production hens are housed in different ways. Many hens are confined to cages giving each bird about an A4 sized piece of paper of personal space. Thankfully in New Zealand, we are in the process of phasing out the caged system. And, I believe the USA is also going cage-free by 2025. However, the caged system is still widely used around the world.

The birds suffer broken bones, feather loss and skin abrasions due to a lifetime confined to a tiny wire cage. Often their beaks are seared off (no anaesthetic) with a hot blade to prevent them pecking at each other from stress, and many hens develop osteoporosis because they are artificially pushed to produce many more eggs than in natural conditions.

Barn raised hens don't fare much better. They are freer, but again, large numbers are kept in the barns with around seven hens per square metre (3.2 sq feet). Like the caged hens, they can have their beaks trimmed and are often kept in dimmed lighting.

Although the barn raised seems to be better than cages a major study done in 2015 of three different hen-housing systems, (cage, colony[6] and barn) found that mortality was highest among birds in barns and that they also had more keel bone problems[7].

Baby chickens, when hatched, are checked for their sex. At one day old the males get thrown alive into a grinder called a macerator, as they are not needed. The ground up result is usually sent off to become pet or fish food. The females are raised under heat lamps until old enough to be sold to the farmers.

Even the free-range sector has a lot to answer for. Their chickens may run free; however, you can guarantee that they have acquired

---

[6] Colony is just another type of wired caged system giving the bird a fraction bit more space, perching availability and one nest box per cage. These can have up to sixty birds per cage, so competition is rife!

[7] The keel bone is the prominent ridge on the sternum of birds to which wing muscles attach

the laying hens through companies employing the sexing method above. Also, these farmers face the same problem as caged hen farmers – what to do with the chicken when it stops laying?

A chicken can normally live around ten to fifteen years; however, their laying ability (especially in the commercial sector) is only about two years. Caged, barn or free-range farmers can't afford to keep their chickens past the laying age … need I say more?

By the way, because both the layer hen and the broiler chicken live in such cramped conditions, they are fed antibiotics. And before you tell me that you only ever have free-range meats and eggs because the animal has a better life, let me say that it is not always the case.

Free-range meat does not necessarily mean the life of the animal is perfect. Chickens can still have their beaks seared off, cows can be dehorned, and pigs can be castrated and painful rings put through their noses. You have to remember that free-range is still farming and the farmer does have to make a living.

Yes, most of the animals do have a better life, but their death is just the same. In fact, some argue that the factory animal at least has just a short life albeit brutal, while the free-range animal lives for longer and is supposedly happier. But at the end of it, the animals endure pain and anguish that is probably far worse for one that has never suffered. The truck journey alone is fearful and confusing for these animals and then to be confronted by the smell of death on arrival at the slaughterhouse must be traumatic for these gentle, cognitive creatures.

Before we end this chapter, I would also like to tell you a little about the organic industry.

Meat that is labelled organic does not mean that the animal has had a good life. Usually far from it. All it means is that the animal has been fed organic food and has not been subjected to antibiotics, hormones or an arsenic-based additive as many non-organic chicken products have.

The animals are still raised in barns or confined spaces. The downside is that, because they don't get the antibiotics, these animals can have all sorts of illness, have a higher mortality rate and be subjected to even more parasites than their drugged counterparts.

So, the idea of free-range and organic as being the ideal meat to have is brought about by the happy chicken, well-fed cow and cute piggy that are portrayed on packaging giving the illusion of well cared for animals. Don't buy into it. It is not necessarily the reality.

Another label to be wary of is 'antibiotic free'. In some countries, all this means is that the animal has had a small period of time before slaughter without antibiotics, so there is no trace of the drug in the meat. Other countries that are stricter have the rule that the animal or bird must be drug-free from day two of its life. So, in the chicken industry in particular, the chickens are fed antibiotics on day one and in a high enough potency to carry them through.

Many countries have no regulations regarding the labelling of free-range. As long as the bird or animal is not caged and barn doors are opened, the meat can be classified as free-range. As mentioned above the chickens grow so quickly that the last few weeks of their life they do not have the physical ability to go outdoors (I am referring to the more extensive corporate operations, not the private farms). The barns are so large that only those chickens on the sidewalls near the openings can get out.

If you want more information on any animal farming methods then search the internet, however, make sure you do a good search – read up on both sides of the arguments and come to your own conclusion. Be prepared for some very shocking and gruesome photos and videos.

Fish

Not only are we depleting our oceans of fish, but we are also destroying the actual oceans as well. I will talk about that in the environment chapter but for now, let me tell you why vegans don't eat fish or go fishing.

One of the most common misconceptions is that fish can't feel pain. It is something that has been debated for years. However, since the early 2000s, fish biologists from around the world have produced substantial evidence that fish experience conscious pain.
Like land animals, they have a central nervous system and the neurons nociceptors. They also produce the same opioids (the natural painkillers) that mammals do.

I'm not going to go into all the experiments that were done on fish, trust me it wasn't at all pleasant. But if you have ever seen a fish being caught and have seen it thrashing around think about what it would be like to have a hook through your mouth and cheek, be pulled through the ocean and end up on a surface where you can't breathe.

As for their intelligence:

> *"Fish are more intelligent than they appear. In many areas, such as memory, their cognitive powers match or exceed those of 'higher' vertebrates including non-human primates."*
>
> *- Culum Brown, Macquarie University*

Studies have found that fish can retain information for months or even years and some fish species are capable of learning complex spatial relationships and forming cognitive maps. They would need this ability as the ocean is such a vast area and fish need to know exactly where they're going. Another indicator of intelligence is that some fish have learned how to use tools which they use for food or building. Some can even make repairs to these tools or creations.

The sad reality is that the way we fish is depleting the oceans of many species which in turn is causing an imbalance as it is eroding the food chain and impacting on many vulnerable species like sea turtles and corals. There is also the bycatch which is the capture of unwanted sea life, causing a needless loss of billions of sea creatures.

It's not just fish either it is all sea life (apart from the sea plants) that are caught or taken for human consumption. The lobster has an intelligence that can rival an octopus and has long been considered to be the smartest invertebrate. They can live for more than 100 years old, have great memories, can recognise other lobsters and, can feel pain. It must be such a violent death to be thrust into a pot of boiling water. It's no wonder the lid has to be held down as the poor thing tries to escape.

Vegans eat neither fish nor crustaceans as they all feel pain, (both the vegans and the sea creatures!).

There is one more 'animal' I'm going to tell you about before we head to the next chapter, and that is the sweet little bee.

Bees

This is one area that is rather grey. A true vegan will not eat honey simply because it is an animal by-product. Actually, vegans will tell you that honey is bee vomit, because of how it's made. Now that is not entirely true.

When the bee collects the pollen, it is stored in an organ called the honey stomach, which is different from the food stomach. Back at the hive, it is then passed onto the worker bee all done via the mouth, hence the word vomit. The worker then passes it along the line, and each one chews it for about half an hour. Gradually it turns into honey. It is then stored in a honeycomb cell, fanned with their wings to get it dry then sealed with a wax lid to keep it clean.

The bees use their honey as food for the long winter months when flowers are scarce.

As you can see, it's quite the process. In fact, it can take eight bees their whole life to make one teaspoon of honey.

Now the bee is an insect with a large nervous system able to transmit pain signals. You can witness this yourself as bees are capable of moving to avoid pain, and they will sting only as a last resort. If you keep perfectly still a bee will not sting you, however, if you jump around it thinks you are attacking it. (And if you are flaying your arms about, you kind of are!),

Those hives that you think are wonderful and where you think the bee is free ... think again. In actual fact, we enslave the bee with those hives and force it to make the honey for our use.

Remember I said that they make the honey to have food over the winter months? Well, in the commercial trade, while they are out working for us, we rob their hives and steal their core products of honey, royal jelly and beeswax. This is done in the autumn, and it leaves the bees without nutrition for the winter. Instead, we feed them on sugar supplements.

The more ethical beekeepers do harvest the honey in the spring, However, there still is the process of actually collecting the honey, and even beekeepers that love and respect their bees still have deaths.

The process begins by smoking the bees. The principal of smoking has been known for thousands of years, but it's only recently that the reason it works has been discovered.

Out in the wild, if a beehive is threatened, guard bees will release a volatile pheromone substance, iso-pentyl acetate, better known as an alarm odour. This alerts the middle-aged bees, (these are the ones with the most venom), to defend the hive by attacking the intruder. Now when smoke is blown into the hive the guard bees' receptors are dulled and they fail to sound the pheromones alarm.

But that's not all. The smoke has a secondary effect in that it causes the other bees to instinctively gorge themselves on honey, which is a survival instinct in case they must vacate the hive and recreate it elsewhere. This gorging has a tendency to pacify the bees.

Now that the bees are calmer, Mr Beekeeper can remove the frames.

Bees get stepped on or squashed by the frames, and of course, the bees that sting the farmer while defending their home also die. It is not on purpose but a hazard of the process of checking the hives and taking the honey.

However, there are other beekeepers that are not so caring about their bees. Just as in the case of factory farming other animals, bees can also be 'factory farmed'.

Humans have apparently been using honey since about 15,000 B.C.; however, it wasn't until the 20th century that it was stepped up into the factory-farming concept that it is today.

In the USA, ten to twenty per cent of colonies are lost over the winter. Some of this is accidental, but most are on purpose.
For some beekeepers, it makes economic sense to kill off their hives before winter. This is usually done by the larger, 'factory-farming' style of beekeeping rather than the small backyard person. One way is to destroy the hives is to seal them up, pour gasoline on them, and set them on fire.

Other ways that the bees can die is when the supers[8] are taken into the warming room that helps to make the honey easier to remove. Bees that come in with the supers are classified as 'stray' bees and are usually disposed of either by being trapped by a wire cone or when there are no windows, an electric grid into which the bees fly.

Here is an abhorrent abusive practice that can occur in the larger honey production units; the wings of the queen bee are cut off so she

---

[8] A honey super consists of a box in which eight to ten frames are hung.

can't leave the colony. She can also be artificially inseminated ... oh yes, she can ... on a bee-sized version of the factory farm 'rape rack'.

There is a newer type of hive that has come onto the market, it is called the flow hive, and the principal is that the hives are never disturbed, but rather the honey flows out via taps.

The secret to it is that the frames are designed so, at the turn of a lever, the little holes making up the 'comb' disconnect, creating channels that the honey flows down and out into a waiting jar.

Once the comb is drained, you turn the lever back which shifts the comb into its original position. Supposedly, the bees then rip off the capping on each cell, repair the cells, and refill them.

All sounds wonderful, and they are saying that it means less stress on the bees and no more pulling out of the frames. However, my research indicates that dedicated beekeepers are saying that there are some flaws.

- The 'window' will get covered by wax; therefore, one cannot see just how much honey is flowing out from the frame. If that happens, how can one gauge how much honey is left for the bees? (Remember, the honey is the bees' food for the winter).
- The hives still have to be checked for disease, swarm prevention, mites, beetles, brood nests etc. So, the smoker still has to be used, and the hive still has to be pulled apart, which means that bees will still be harmed and killed.

- The Flow hive is a plastic comb hive which, according to several beekeepers, bees hate plastic, it is toxic, the bees take longer to wax it and also it is an environmental hazard if burned.

- Having honey out in a jar on the outside of the hive can make it susceptible to robbing. *Robbing* is a situation in which a beehive is attacked by invaders from other hives ... the robbers are after the honey. Therefore, having jars outside the hive collecting the honey may promote the honey robbing between hives.

- To get the honey to 'flow' the weather needs to be warm, which begs the question of what happens in the cooler areas when crystallisation or granulation happens to the honey?

One more thing that I discovered. It is so much better if the bees are allowed to create their hives naturally. As I've said above, bees don't particularly like plastic. Ask any organic beekeeper. They don't need it. They fashion wax – a living substance – out of their own abdomens. Wax is where they store their food (nectar and pollen) and house their young.

Beekeeper Jonathan Powell, who has a long family connection with bees, and is also a partner with a UK Charity called the Natural Bee-keeping Trust, said:

> *"The (honey) comb is far more than a Tupperware container for somebody else's lunch; it is the tissue and frame of the hive, and as such, it forms multiple functions."*

Now is it good for the bees? Who cares?

We've got flowing honey.

Honey is so easy to get off the supermarket shelf that we forget just how much the bees have to go through and suffer for our taste buds.

The sad part is that bees are in decline. They are literally dying off and, if we don't do something about it soon, we will be facing very dire consequences. There are two things that seem to be causing this. They are being attacked by a viral infection, and they are perilously vulnerable to pesticides.

A study to come out of Harvard University published June 2014 in the Bulletin of Insectology shows that neonicotinoids are killing bees[9] at an exponential rate. Neonicotinoids are the world's most widely used insecticides and are the direct cause of the phenomenon labelled as Colony Collapse Disorder or CCD

Unfortunately, there is nothing we can do other than stop spraying!!!! But regardless whether we're eating the honey or not, the bees are still dying.

Vegans find this situation intolerable.

Luckily there are many things that can replace honey as a sweetener.

Rice syrup

Molasses

Sorghum

Barley malt

Maple syrup – (my favourite)

Cane or coconut sugar

Dates - (the one I usually use.)

Using these will keep your diet bee-free.

Governments continue to bury their heads. It was even muted in Britain that after Brexit animals would no longer be classified as

---

[9] Other pollinating insects are also being killed by neonicotinoids.

sentient completely undoing all the good that has been achieved in the European Union. At the time of writing, this had not come into law, but it certainly is a scary thought that the animal agriculture industry could have that much sway over a government as to re-introduce such an archaic belief.

Every day more evidence emerges about the horror of the animal food industry machine. What these animals have to endure is beyond comprehension to the majority and if it were not for the animal activists and organisations like PETA and here in New Zealand SAFE a lot of people would still be unaware.

However, with the rise of social media, more documentaries being made, and corporations producing vegan foods all bodes well for the future.

4 – The Hidden Cruelty

I want you to stop for a minute and have a look at the shoes you're wearing. Are they leather? What about the woolly jersey or hat? Maybe you even have a silk scarf or tie? Perhaps you have some honey in your pantry? What about make-up, shampoo, cleaners, medications? Have you been to a rodeo lately, or been to the races? Perhaps you've visited a zoo or taken a ride on an elephant? Many of these things impact on animals, so this chapter is dedicated to them, the quite often forgotten animals who give their lives for our convenience, entertainment and experiments.

I'm going to divide this chapter into three parts.
Using animals for:
- What we wear.
- Entertainment.
- Vivisection (experiments).

All three are a part of the vegan's ethical beliefs, and so this is an integral part of the lifestyle.

What we wear.

Let's being with
Leather.

How wonderful is it to go into a shoe shop and try on a beautiful pair of Italian or Brazilian shoes? Wearing comfortable and fashionable footwear from countries that supply high, designer brands seem to be the ultimate in luxury.

Then again, maybe you can't afford that high quality, and so you stick with the 'Made In A Country That Has Cheap Labour and Cheap Leather' shoes'.

And what about those glorious handbags you have or the leather couch you may be sitting on? What's the fabric your car seats are made from, could it be leather? Leather is a fabric that is found literally everywhere.

To jog your memory, here's a list of leather goods and rest assured that it doesn't contain everything:

Clothing	Shoes
Belts	Hats and Gloves
Luggage	Brief Cases
Glasses cases	Luggage labels
Key Fobs	Diaries & journals
Writing compendiums	Wallets
Builders' pouch	Watch straps
Bridles	Smithy aprons
Harnesses	Saddles
Pet collars	Furniture
Car upholstery	Leads
Desk tops	Chamois
Jewellery	… and more and more

Have a look around your house. Any leather? Suede? Animal skins? I'd be surprised if there is none unless you have already gone leather-free. Some leather is absolutely unavoidable as it is a material that is used in so many different ways. It can be found in sports equipment, tools, used in bookbinding, and sometimes even hidden from view such as within the framework of furniture.

Have you ever wondered where the leather comes from? Maybe you have, or maybe you haven't. Either way, perhaps there is so much leather around that you don't even really think about it, or perhaps you just turn a blind eye.

So, I'm about to educate you. And, at the end of this chapter, if you're still going to buy leather shoes or bags, then you are obviously not cut out to be a vegan.

I'm sure that by now you're an avid supporter of banning the fur trade. Even Queen Elizabeth, in 2019, committed to cease buying animal fur instead will buy fake fur. It will be interesting to see if she avoids wearing any of the fur coats and stoles she already has.

I'd even go so far as to say that you think the fur trade is barbaric and there is no way you would ever even consider buying something made with fur. Good for you if you think this way. You are so totally right in knowing that it is a barbaric trade.

More than 1 billion rabbits and 50 million other animals world-wide are trapped or farmed expressly for the fashion fur industry. There is no reason to use fur anymore even if you do live in the coldest of cold countries. There are other options that do not include an animal.

Eighty-five per cent of the fur is farmed. And seriously, life for these animals is a living hell. The animals involved are rabbits, foxes, raccoon dogs, mink and chinchillas and the farms are designed to make maximum profits, so the welfare of the animal is at a minimum.

The animals are in small wire cages generally with food paste being put through the top and excrement passed through the wire floor and left to pile up underneath. Sometimes more than one animal is in the cage. Just like other factory-farmed animals, they are unable to express their species-specific behaviour. The cramped conditions cause severe welfare issues such as circling and pacing, fur chewing and even self-injury all caused by frustration.

There are different ways the animals are killed. Two of the worst are gassing and head to tail electrocution as just a couple. Gassing for Mink is highly brutal as they are semi-aquatic and can hold their breath. This means they are highly tolerant to low levels of oxygen and can suffer significantly during the gassing procedure.

The electrocution method is horrific too as electrodes are put in both the mouth and the anus, causing severe pain and distress to the animal. As the farmer does not want any damage done to the pelt, other methods are neck-breaking, bludgeoning or hanging. Even being skinned alive is another way of getting the hide as videos from Asia have shown. One billion rabbits are killed every year for clothing, or craft items or even for lures in fly fishing.

Trapping is another cruel and inhumane way of catching animals. Around the world, the traps include steel-jaw leg-hold traps (probably the most common), body-gripping traps and wire neck snares. All are designed to hold the animal and not kill it. However, it is extremely painful, and animals will sometimes even chew off their own limb to get free. Many other non-target animals are caught in these traps, and they are considered to be trash and so discarded. It is estimated that between one and ten of these 'trash' animals are caught for every one targeted animal.

Then we have the seal fur trade. In 2016, over 66,000 seal pups were killed for their fur, genitalia (used in China as an aphrodisiac), and Omega 3 oils (used in supplements). The seals can be between 12 days and 12 months old, and many are skinned alive or left to die after being clubbed until the hunter can get back to skin it.

There is slowly a realisation going on in the fashion industry that fur is not a fashion statement any more. Many designers are ditching the fur and using 'fake fur' instead and by 2019 some of the largest fashion houses and large department stores had ditched fur.

> *"There is no kind way to rip the skin off animals' backs. Anyone who wears any fur shares the blame for the torture and gruesome deaths of millions of animals each year."*
> *- Natalie Imbruglia*

The fur trade is specific, and it is good to see the fur trade declining. However, there is still a long way to go if we are to see animals out of fashion altogether.

We have been led to believe, leather is a by-product of the meat industry and that if the skins are not used for leather, they are wasted. So, most people, even meat-eaters who are totally against the fur trade, don't understand at all that the leather trade is just as cruel and barbaric.

Most of the leather sold comes from animals that are specifically killed for their skins, and the meat is more the by-product. You see the skin of the cow is around ten per cent of the cow's value, which actually makes it the most profitable part.

Here's something I'm sure you won't know. India is one of the world's biggest producers of leather. Sixty-five per cent of its leather and leather goods are exported, and there are over 2,000 tanneries scattered around India.

I couldn't find any recent facts about the leather industry in India; however, I did come across an Indian Government paper that stated:

> "...There exists a large raw material base. This is on account of population of 194 million cattle, 70 million buffaloes, 95 million goats. According to the latest census, India ranks first among the major livestock holding countries in the world. In respect of sheep with 48 million sheep, it claims the sixth position. These four species provide the basic raw material for leather industry....."

I do wonder what the figures are today, I know they have slipped down the ladder, and now China takes the number one title of exporting leather producing nearly 372,000 square metres (four billion square feet) each year. Following close behind is Brazil and then Italy with around 139,000 square metres (1.5 billion square feet). India is equal to Russia although Russia's leather production is declining

Now, you're probably thinking that it is rather strange that India has such a high rate of leather considering the fact that most of the population are Hindu and regard cows as sacred. In fact, cows are supposed to be allowed to die a natural death and then, at that point, are available for their skins. The downward trend in the leather trade has been mainly due to the Hindu government coming down hard on abattoirs and tanneries that are run by Muslims. This is causing leading consumer brands to go elsewhere like to China, Bangladesh, Indonesia and Pakistan. So, even if India's leather trade has plummeted, the other countries have scored very well as leather goods are such mainstay commodities.

And just as an aside, the Indian federal government tried to ban the trade of cattle for slaughter citing cruelty to animals, sadly that was overturned, and the animal cruelty continues. Just one example is when cows are being herded onto over-crowded trucks or made to walk between trucking points. They are beaten and forced to move by having chilli seeds rubbed into their eyes and their tails broken. This type of practice has increased due to the different States banning the killing, and so the animals are taken to States that still allow it.

But it's not only the cows that suffer and are used for the leather industry. Take a look at the other animals also used:
Goats, pigs, sheep and lambs, horses, deer, kangaroos, snakes, alligators and crocodiles, elephants, zebras, bison, water buffalo, boars and pigs, eels, sharks, dolphins, seals, walruses, frogs, turtles, and lizards. Then, of course, there's calf both born and unborn, ostriches, dogs and cats.

Did you also see that I had included in the list unborn calf? This is called 'slink', a leather that is very soft and is very prized. It can come from cows, sheep, deer, or pretty much any animal but the usual slinks come from the calf of a cow. Those calves we talked about earlier, the ones that are aborted from the dairy cow. Sometimes the farmer will sell the foetus, as it is valued for its hide. Another source is pregnant cows that are sent to slaughter. In New Zealand, pregnant cows are meant to have birthed the calf before being killed. Sadly, this doesn't always happen. These 'mistakes' can be used for slink leather.

Now if all this so far isn't enough.

Let's look at alligators farmed in the USA. These animals can typically live to the age of 60 years, but the farmed ones are generally killed before they reach the age of two. This is because the optimum time to harvest is calculated on their length rather than their age. How do you kill an alligator? Pretty much just beat it to death with a mallet and axe. Tragically, alligators can still be alive after they are skinned and can remain conscious for several hours.

Snakes, such as the boa constrictor and cobra, are skinned alive, as it is believed that will make the skin softer. Due to their slow metabolism, they can still live on in absolute agony for up to two or more days.

In Australia, millions of kangaroos are killed every year. This is regarded as the most massive land-based slaughter of wildlife in the world.

The kangaroo is supposed to be killed with a single shot according to the Industry Code of Practice. That's laughable. There is absolutely no way that this can be monitored. Every single night in remote locations there are vehicles approaching kangaroos, blinding them with spotlights and shooting without worrying too much about the 'single-shot' rule. It is estimated that about 440,000 dependent young kangaroos are either clubbed to death or left to starve after their mothers are killed.

Along with shoes and accessories, kangaroo leather is also used in the manufacture of sporting shoes, including soccer boots. It was great to see that David Beckham back in 2006, switched to synthetic materials when he learned of the cruel killing methods.

Now, it seems to me that if any creature has a skin, it is fair game for the leather market because there will be a human somewhere who will want to wear it.

Leather also impacts on other things besides the killing of the animal. The environment and the health of the humans who work and/or live near the tanneries.

The manufacturing of the hides produces waste matter such as dust, hair, trimmings and shavings. Then, of course, there is the effluent, which comes in large volumes. Contaminated with toxic compounds such as aluminium, chromium sulphide and caustic soda both the solid waste and the effluent are often discharged into rivers and waterways causing severe pollution.

Tanneries usually are near rivers, as they require a constant supply of water. The breakdown of the waste demands high oxygen, which, in turn, disturbs the ecological balance of the area. By stripping oxygen from the water, plants, bacteria and fish die, which leads to a growth of toxic, polluted water and significant health issues of the surrounding population.

Equally sad is that many people who work in or live near tanneries are dying from cancer that is caused by exposure to the toxic chemicals.

Morocco, in North Africa, has one of the oldest tanneries in the world and is renowned for its colourful soft leather. What makes the tanning process there unusual is that every stage is completed by hand (or foot!), and in the harshest of conditions: in a hot climate, with the bare minimum of wages, where even sometimes child labour is involved. The workers seem to be solely male, and you can see them move between the stone vessels effectively dyeing their own skins with a multitude of colours.

However, all of this is nothing compared to the drifting odour that hangs around the place. Most tanneries are surrounded by homes which means that local occupants must tolerate one of the most unbearable smells known to man – that of the wet, putrid, stinking hide. And all in the name of creating beautiful leather goods.

Even discarded leather products decompose slowly, usually taking up to 50 years, mainly because of the preservation treatment it had during manufacturing. During this time, it can leech chemicals into the earth, and this is one of the reasons some vegans will buy recycled leather goods from thrift stores etc. This is a personal choice and one that you must make on your own. However, no vegans will purchase brand new leather goods.

It's about now that I'm going to mention snakeskin. Obviously, there are many different animals that have their skins removed or are farmed in cruel conditions, but snakeskin is simply abhorrent.

The number one snake used is the python. This is because it has a large area of skin. Other snakes used are Indian or Asian cobra, water snake, boa constrictor, king snake, anaconda, viper, vine or whip snake and rattlesnake.

The python is a protected species and is supposed to be obtained from farms, but just as many are hunted in Indonesia and Malaysia. The snakes are getting smaller and smaller in number, and the hunters have to travel further to get them. The species is really threatened. Once captured, their heads are cut off by a machete. Now, because snakes have a slow metabolism, their bodies remain conscious, and even though they have had their heads removed, they still feel pain for some time after.

Another horrific practice is to nail the snake's head to a tree and skin it alive then it is thrown onto a heap with others where it can take up to two days to die. If that's not enough, another method is to put a tube down their throat and pump them up with water. The neck is then tied with rope to stop fluid escaping, and they are hung up. They can be left hanging, bloated and suffering for more than ten minutes before they are slit open, end to end, and the skin is ripped off. Once the skin is off, they are thrown onto the pile with other dying snakes.

The skins that are shed naturally are too thin for the fashion industry so snakes must die in order for someone to wear python or rattlesnake boots or any other fashion accessory.

There are many alternatives to all animal skins available both natural, such as hemp and bamboo, and synthetic. Cruelty-free stores like MooShoes, Beyond Skin, Vegan Essentials, Alternative Outfitters and Vaute Couture can be found on the Internet.

When buying anything at all, just like with food, read the label. Try and support ethical companies that care about animals and the environment.

I want to mention here that dogs and cats are also farmed for leather. As I mentioned before, China is now the world's leading exporter of leather, and it is estimated that approximately two million dogs and cats are skinned annually for the trade. The downside is that consumers purchase this leather unknowingly because of mislabelling and inaccurate indications of the origin. Using these animals is also increasing in India due to the government crack-down on the cattle trade.

It doesn't matter if the shoes or bag is inexpensive or coming from a high-end fashion label if it says 'made in China' there is now a much higher chance it is made from dog skin as this trade is increasing at an alarming rate.

I had a friend recently who purchased a pair of leather shoes online. She told me that she chose these particular ones because they were made in Italy and she felt that, not only would the leather have come from a good source, (although what she meant by that I totally failed to understand), but also no sweatshop would have been used.

However, when they arrived, she looked inside them and there stamped on the leather was 'made in China'. She was rather outraged, but more because of the false advertising rather than the leather. Needless to say, I did comment "Oh my, that's such a shame, now you don't know if the leather is actually from a cow. If it's made in China, it could be a dog or a cat!"

She gasped at that comment and looked at me horrified. Now she was not only outraged but disgusted too. Sadly, she didn't see the irony of what I'd said. What I fail to understand is, what's the difference if it is a dog or a cow? The animal died for her shoes.

Dog skins - China

It is an industry that is becoming more prevalent for several reasons but mainly because dogs and cats are easier to farm than large cows.

We have been so ingrained in the idea that some animals are respected and loved and other animals are just there for us to use in whatever way we choose. We have become desensitized to the murder, just like the worker who throws those baby boy chickens into the grinder.

Now let's take a look at

Wool.

Different countries have different laws governing the treatment of sheep. The main one being mulesing. This is a barbaric practice that has now been banned in all major wool-exporting countries, including South Africa, Uruguay, Argentina, Canada, the USA and New Zealand. However, it is still very much legal in the largest wool exporting country, Australia.

It may be banned from these other countries, but they are still able to import mulesed wool, so there's a real contradiction in ethics. There is one bright spot though, about sixty international retailers, most of who are in Europe, actually have boycotted Australian wool.

What is mulesing? It supposedly controls flystrike on the rear end of the sheep. It is especially done on Merino sheep that have been bred to have wrinkly skin specifically to get more wool.

It is performed by forcing the sheep onto its back, restraining its legs between metal bars and then carving off large chunks of skin from the backside.

The other way is attaching vice-like clamps to the flesh until it dies and sloughs off. Neither procedure is done with any type of anaesthetic, and both are very painful. Over 20 million sheep each year have this done to them!

The silly part is that it is not a procedure that is necessary. There are other ways to prevent flystrike. Even sheep that have been bred to have unwrinkled hindquarters, called bare-breech sheep, are now available to farmers, but the practice of mulesing continues.

Other things that happen in the sheep industry are to the lambs. These are docking, (removing the tails), and castration, (removing the testicles), both performed without anaesthetic and usually without painkillers even though it is recommended.

The whole problem is that the sheep have been bred to have thick woollen coats. In the wild, the woolly coat is shed around springtime, or it only grows to a certain length, thus wild sheep do not have to be shorn.

The shearing process itself can be a painful experience. Shearers are usually paid by the number of sheep shorn not the number of hours worked. This can mean that they can rush to get as many sheep shorn as possible.

Unfortunately, struggling sheep can be brutally punched and inexperienced or careless shearers who are in a hurry can injure parts of the sheep, such as the face or even cut the end of a teat off.

The sheep are usually sheared once a year in the spring quite often just before lambs are born. In the colder areas, spring does not necessarily mean warmer weather and some sheep can die from exposure to the cold.

Oh, and speaking of lambs. Sheep generally only have one lamb. Now it is quite common to see twins and triplets, which is more a result of genetic selection, intensive feeding or the use of hormones and other drugs.

Under normal circumstances, sheep can live for around fifteen years, but because their wool production falls off, the sheep are slaughtered or even sent off to other countries as 'live export' around the age of seven.

The exports of these sheep are generally to countries in the Middle East and North Africa where there are no animal welfare laws. Most of these animals are killed by having their throats slit while they are still conscious. Many sheep die on the voyage from hunger, dehydration, overcrowding or heat stress. Some countries have now banned the export of live sheep.

Before we leave the wool industry, there are a couple more things to look at.

A significant proportion of British wool is from already slaughtered sheep, and this is referred to as 'skin wool'.

Fifty per cent of the world's mohair wool comes from angora goats in South Africa. Recent investigative footage from the mohair industry in South Africa shows appalling abuse on these beautiful animals.
It shows the goats being roughly sheared, with gaping wounds sewn shut without anaesthetic. It also showed goats killed by beheading with a dull knife.
No one should be wearing or using any item that is made from the hair of these gentle animals. They are left bloody and terrified after having been held down and shorn.

Wool is found in a variety of things besides clothing. It plays quite a big part in the baby industry in such items as swaddle blankets, baby wraps, blankets, infant sleeping bags and outer covers for cloth diapers. As well as lining shoes/slippers it is also used as a warm mattress cover for colder climates and can be used as a soil fertilizer, being a slow-release source of nitrogen. It is used to make felt which leads to another industry and also to absorb odours and noise in heavy machinery and stereo speakers along with home insulation products. And of course, there is the upholstery and carpet manufacturing that we all know about.

One thing that is beneficial about merino wool is that it is a perfect fabric to use for firefighters' uniforms. It has a flame retardant up to 600 degrees centigrade. At these high temperatures, it doesn't shrink or melt, which means it doesn't stick to the skin plus it has no toxic odours. However, that being said, many firefighters' uniforms are made with Kevlar® fibre and engineered with Nomex®. This synthetic fibre which works similar to merino, was created in the mid-1960s and was first used commercially in the 1970s, so you see, there is no excuse to use wool.

Lanolin, also called wool wax or wool grease, is secreted by the sebaceous glands. Lanolin is extracted by washing the wool in hot water with a special wool scouring detergent to remove dirt, wool grease (crude lanolin), suint (sweat salts), and anything else stuck to the wool. Then it is refined more by using an alkaline treatment and alcohol. The more it is refined, the purer it gets.

One of the medicinal uses of lanolin is in the manufacture of Vitamin D. Because it is an animal product, it contains D3 that is more potent than the D2 found in plants. Vegan Registered Dietician Brenda Davis provides a comprehensive yet easy-to-read explanation of Vitamin D, including a discussion of the differences between D2 and D3. Her conclusion is simple:

> *"… vegans who seek out vitamin D2 in order to avoid animal products may need to consume greater amounts to get the same benefit as what is provided by vitamin D3."*

Taking a vitamin D supplement is something I do and always recommend it to everyone, not just vegans.

Because of lanolin's protective qualities, it is commonly used in cosmetic creams and lotions designed to smooth and moisturise the skin. Probably the closest we can get to lanolin is cocoa butter. It melts at a high degree and then when cooled is malleable just like lanolin.

Other products you can look for to use instead are aloe, olive oil, coconut oil, cocoa butter, vitamin E oil, almond oil, or grapeseed oil.

Of course, there are many other animals used in the fashion trade that you might be wearing:

Angora – rabbit fur
Alpaca fleece – alpaca
Mohair – angora goats
Cashmere – cashmere goats
Silk – silkworm
Camelhair – camel
Doeskin – deer or even lambskin
Felt – matted animal fibres
Haircloth – horse or camel hair (used for upholstery)
Velvet – can be made from a variety of animal fibres
Down – duck and geese feathers

Feathers
So now that I've mentioned the duck and geese feathers let's talk about these. You know that gorgeous down duvet or comforter you have on your bed? What about the feather pillow? Have you any

idea how the down/feathers were harvested from the duck or goose?

Most people think that feathers come as a by-product from the poultry industry and, to a point, that is true; however, it's not always the case.

In some countries, it is still legal to physically pluck the feathers from the poultry while the bird is still alive. Generally, birds moult once or twice a year. In the feather market, the process is repeated every six to seven weeks meaning that the bird is not necessarily ready to moult. The most common way is to hold the duck or goose by the neck or wings and literally rip the down feathers out. Now because the bird is not ready to moult the skin will tear and then be sewn up without anaesthetic and the bird is left to heal. With the feather harvest happening so often the birds die either from the trauma of it all or the feathers diminish and so they are sent to slaughter.

I personally rate this as one of the top barbaric practices done to birds.

There's one last fabric to mention.

Silk.

So many people have really no idea where silk comes from, and that includes vegans. It's one of those fabrics that most believe is perfectly all right.

Silk originated in China around 3000BC. Apparently, Lady Hsi-Ling-Shih, the wife of the mythical Yellow Emperor, was given the title 'Goddess of Silk'. The story goes that after discovering the silkworm in the wild and the fabric it could make, she introduced silkworm rearing and the loom on which the silk was spun.

Silk stayed in China until the Silk Road opened up around 130 BC, and then the fabric started to be traded. But it was centuries later before other countries began to cultivate the silkworm and that's when the production of silk expanded.

So how is it made? The silk is the protein fibre found in the larvae of certain insects. The most well-known is the larvae of the silkworm Bombyx Mori found on mulberry and, as there are none left in the wild, they are all reared in captivity.

The silkworm never gets to be fully grown because it is the cocoon that is needed. These cocoons are thrown live into boiling water with the little worm still inside. You could say a smaller version of how crayfish are cooked.

The fabric needed to make a single sari can take up to 50,000 cocoons.

There is a new technique that does not require killing the worm. An Indian man, Kusuma Rahaiah, has developed this technique[10] and has the patent for making 'ahimsa' silk. Mind you, the production is more expensive, so not quite within the reach of most people. ... yet. It all sounds rather excellent until you delve a little deeper and discover that the cocoons may be empty, but the moths are killed as they are classified as a by-product and not needed.

There has been a lot of inbreeding going on, and over the generations, the bodies of the moths that emerge are far too heavy in proportion to their wings – unable to move, let alone fly. Perhaps it is a blessing that they are crushed to death in a mixer. Seems to be quite a standard practice for small beings, think baby chicks.

Obviously, some females are kept, and male moths are stored in a refrigerator and only taken out for mating. This happens two or three times or until the male is no longer useful at which stage it is then discarded into the trash and left just to wither away and die.

Neither method is ethically vegan — both kill the animal at some point in its life, and both are still using animals for our own purpose when there are other fabrics to choose from.

Did you know that materials such as chiffon, damask, flannel, and crepe and even some gabardine could be made from animal?

Cruelty-free fabrics do exist, and they are not hard to find. You will get used to knowing which materials are animal-free the more you embrace the vegan lifestyle. You will also discover that there are some gorgeous vegan options.

---

[10] Apparently, there is a company in Oregon that already uses this technique, it's called Peace Silk.

Material to look out for:

Hemp – can be used for shoes or clothing, very versatile.

Bamboo – this makes beautiful fabric.

Jute – great for shoes and bags.

Cotton – organic cotton is the one to choose as the normal cotton is sprayed with the highest amount of pesticides of all the crops in the world.

Soy – this can be as soft as cashmere.

Lyocell – this is made from wood, yes, wood. Although not organic, it is far less damaging to the environment than polyester. Can be used to replace suede, satin and silk.

Speaking of polyester and nylon, both of which is man-made and vegan, below is the reason why I have not added them to the list.

Made from petrochemicals, these synthetics are non-biodegradable as well, so they are inherently unsustainable on two counts. Nylon manufacture creates nitrous oxide, a greenhouse gas 310 times more potent than carbon dioxide. Making polyester uses large amounts of water for cooling, which, along with lubricants, can become a source of contamination. Both processes are also very energy-hungry.

But, never fear, there are amazing vegan choices in clothes and other accessories. As I mentioned earlier, buying clothes made of animal products through thrift stores, garage or yard sales or any other recycling method is very much a personal choice. If you take on the vegan lifestyle, you don't necessarily have to throw out clothes you already have but with new items, definitely be looking at the labels of clothes, shoes, bags and anything else to see what its made of before you purchase it.

Shopping online can be a very good way of getting around having to look at labels as you can go directly to places that sell just vegan clothes or accessories.

There are several apps that can be downloaded for free onto your smartphone that will give you help and guidance in choosing what is vegan and what is not — giving you companies that do not test on animals and products in the cosmetic range that are vegan.

But if you are shopping in the traditional way, then you certainly will be reading labels for everything!

If you're into designer labels and fashion houses, here is a list of those who do not use animal and are cruelty-free.

Stella McCartney

John Bartlett

Leanne Mai-luy Hilgart (started Vaute Couture)

Joshua Katcher (Brave Gentlemen)

Vivienne Westwood

Tommy Hilfiger

Calvin Klein

Charlotte Ronson

Marc Bouwer

And those who have ditched the fur:

Burberry

John Galliano

DKNY

Versace

Michael Kors (and as he now owns the Jimmy Choo brand, not there either.)

Gucci

Giorgio Armani

Ralph Lauren

Calvin Klein

There are some big names there and this where we will see the change when more fashion houses and designers get the message, you don't need to use animals to be fashionable.

Just one more point before we leave the clothes on their hangers. Another thing rather high on the priority list, for a lot of vegans, is finding clothes that are ethically made by manufacturers who don't employ children, offer work safe environments and pay a decent wage. Vegan and ethical clothing, especially shoes, can be expensive, which is why the recycled way is a very viable option.

Entertainment.

We all know about zoos and aquariums, and I'm sure you think there is a real need for us to have them, right? Yes, they are different today in so far as in the past the animal, (and I'm including marine life in this), were put on display for our entertainment. The WAZA, (World Association of Zoos and Aquariums), state that:

> "*these places must be centres for animal welfare and must ensure that the conditions for the animals in their care are the best that can be delivered*".

Sadly, this isn't always the case.

Free Willy was a profound movie that began a movement to stop the training and displaying of Orcas in captivity. San Diego SeaWorld was targeted, not only because it probably was top of the priority list for tourists, but because of the small tanks and obvious distress the Orcas suffered. This culminated in the documentary, Black Fish which highlighted the problem of all aquariums around the world, and since then, through demonstrations and lobbying, SeaWorld has stopped their breeding program. However, they continue to 'entertain the crowds' with the Orcas they still have, and it may be decades before that comes to an end.

However, by the end of the first decade, there were a number of companies and airlines who removed Sea World from their list of tourist destinations, a move applauded by activists and vegans worldwide.

Aquatic Entertainment

I think we can all agree that no aquatic mammals should be in aquariums, especially when they usually have very little space relative to the ocean they came from. Plus, how these Orcas and Dolphins are found for these facilities is cruel and heartless. Taiji Cove, Japan, (an excellent documentary, The Cove, was made about this place), has a dolphin hunt once a year. Dolphins are herded into the cove and many, especially the young and albino, are captured for the live trade to become performing exhibits in aquariums.

The rest are butchered for the meat market, leaving the water red with blood. Please note, this happens in other places throughout Japan and other parts of the world, but the Taiji Cove slaughter is one that is known worldwide.

At the beginning of 2019, AFD (Action for Dolphins) filed a legal action again the Taiji dolphin hunts. This was a world-first. It was fronted by Ren Yabuki, director of the animal protection charity, Life Investigation Agency. He was the plaintiff and had a team of Japanese lawyers who took the dolphin hunters to court. The legal action was filed against the Governor of Wakayama Prefecture who signs the permits allowing the hunts.

Basically, the lawsuit was that the fishermen violated Japan's animal welfare laws and violated the catch quotas allowed on their permits.

After three hearings, the judge dismissed the case on legal standing. However, there are plans to take the case to the High Court in 2020.

The tanks that most of these sea mammals are kept in are far too small. Orcas and dolphins are still trained to perform for the crowds, and it is now well documented that they can develop mental illnesses from the confinement. Trainers have been killed while interacting with these beautiful mammals. The famous orca, Tilikum, from

SeaWorld in San Diego, killed one trainer and was a party to three other deaths.

But the trade continues around the world with dolphins, orcas, penguins and other sea life being held in captivity. One could argue that, because of global warming and the seas changing, it is better for these animals to be in the confines of these marine parks. But it is an artificial environment, and the animals do not live the length of time they would in the wild.

The only bright light is The Whale Sanctuary Project. This is an organisation that focuses exclusively on creating sanctuaries in North America for orcas, beluga whales and dolphins. A place they can retire to or come to if rescued. This will mean that these beautiful mammals will not be confined to concrete tanks for the rest of their lives (which could be thirty to forty years) but will be free to swim in ocean waters and have a vast area to roam.

The Zoo

For land animals, it's a similar situation. Although many zoos are continually upgrading their facilities, they still cannot provide the space that wild animals need, especially for those that would typically roam vast distances in their natural habitat.

A government-funded study of elephants in the U.K. zoos found that 54 per cent of the elephants showed behavioural problems during the daytime. One elephant observed during day and night had behaviour issues for 61 per cent over a 24-hour period. Lions and other big cats spend a good portion of their time pacing, as they don't have space.

Many thousands of healthy animals are killed in zoos for all sorts of different reasons, culling being just one. In early 2015 there was worldwide outrage when a healthy young giraffe was killed because it was unsuitable for breeding. To make matters worse, his body was dissected in front of the public, including children, and then fed to the lions.

Zoos, it is argued, are there to help stop the extinction of animals. Granted there are some animals that no longer exist in the wild but can still be found in Zoos. This is such a sad indictment of our human species that we are destroying animals, including ourselves, in what is known as the Sixth Extinction.

Animals are still being used for entertainment around the world. However, more countries are coming on board with a ban. Sadly, some of those bans only include animals caught in the wild, so animals bred within captured environments like zoos are still able to be sold to circuses.

Circus animals are kept in confined cages or are chained travelling for eleven months a year in box cars without temperature control, nor separate spaces for sleeping, eating and defecating. The training is often brutal and dangerous. The methods can include the use of beating clubs, electric prods, bull hooks and deprivation of food.

The racing industry.
This is another area that is abusive to animals. Even here in New Zealand, we have our fair share of horses having to be put down right there on the racetrack. There's no denying that drugs are used especially painkillers or, even cocaine, to disguise the pain the horse might feel during races. Dog racing also has a massively high death rate due to injuries or because most can't be re-homed. One man I spoke to recently who has a rescue greyhound said that rules around

dog racing are very 'loose' and many dogs just 'go missing' ... an industry term for killing off those dogs who are past their racing prime.

This is just touching on some of the so-called entertainment we force animals into in order to satisfy a day's 'fun'. Other types are:

Rodeo

Bullfighting

Cockfighting

Hunting

Fishing

Camel and elephant rides

And the latest on the agenda for the tourist is the selfie. Taken with tigers who have been so drugged up they are calm enough for the tourist to sit right beside them. They endure a lifetime of suffering starting from when they are taken from their mothers at a very young age, followed by unrelenting handling and stressful interactions with visitors. They are confined to small cages, chained and subjected to harsh training. This is not the life for an animal as beautiful as the tiger.

No animal is on this planet for our entertainment.

Vivisection.

The word vivisection means:

> *"the practice of performing operations on live animals for the purpose of experimentation or scientific research"*

It is a term used by those who are against any form of animal testing that goes on around the world in the name of science, medicine and beauty.

In 2018 the Japanese killed over three hundred minke whales and fifty whales in an Antarctic protected area all under their 'scientific' program. They have since come out and declared that they would be openly whaling, hunting for the domestic food market, although only in the seas they control, (as if that's going to help the whales!).

So, under the guise of 'scientific research' how would you feel if I told you that an estimated twenty-six million animals die every year in the USA alone, and 100 million are tested on.

Now don't think other countries don't test because over 300,000 animals die here in New Zealand and six million die in Australia. I don't have the figures for the U.K., Europe or China but they all test. These tests are done to develop medical treatments and determine the toxicity of medications. Then there are the tests to check to see if a product is going to be safe for humans.

The animals that get tested on are monkeys, dogs, rabbits, rats and mice and also pigs, cows, deer, fish and birds and guinea pigs – the list goes on - it's like no animal is exempt.

In most countries, animal testing is mandatory before any product can be let loose on the public. Some countries have banned cosmetic testing but will still test for medical and scientific purposes. Like here in New Zealand, we don't do cosmetic testing, but if a New Zealand company wants to export to China, they have to prove the product has been animal tested. In 2019 China did announce that it was moving towards alternative tests that don't involve animals. On this announcement, a few companies stopped testing their products destined for China, but they still have to pay the Chinese government to get the tests done. Either way, the animals still lose.

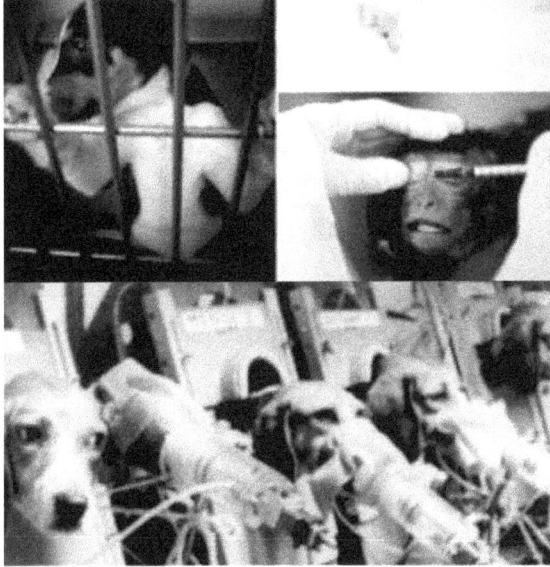

In the U.K., there is a call for the government to stop testing on primates. It serves little value and causes immense suffering. In fact, a study done in 2016 showed that the cruel experiments done on monkeys' brains were useless as they were flawed and served little value.

Why?

Because there are some rather significant differences between a monkey brain and a human brain. Sadly, as of the date of writing, the U.K. government refuses to even address this practice at all.

Some experiments use the 50/50 rule. This means that 50 percent of the animals are given as much of the substance as necessary to get them to die or close to death and the other 50 percent are given enough to see if there is a reaction.

Animals are force fed, forced to breathe toxic substances, they may have food and water deprivation, prolonged periods of physical restraint, infliction of burns and other wounds to study the healing process, the infliction of pain to study its effects and remedies, injected with toxic substances, given diseases and, when the experiment ends, they are killed by carbon dioxide asphyxiation, neck-breaking, decapitation, or other means.

The Draize eye test, in particular, is very nasty. Cosmetic companies use it to evaluate irritation caused by shampoos and other products. It involves rabbits being put into stocks with their eyelids held open by clips, so they cannot blink away the products being tested. Once the injuries are recorded, the rabbits are killed. And if you've ever had a bit of shampoo in your eye, you'll know that it's not nice. Next time it happens, remember a rabbit has had the prototype formula in its eyes, so you don't get the stinging or burning sensation.

There are other ways to test. Studying cell cultures in a petri dish actually can produce more relevant results because human cells are used. Then there is Microdosing, which is used on human volunteers. It is the administration of doses too small to cause adverse reactions. The dose is given, then the blood is analysed. There is also artificial human skin which is commercially available. It's made from sheets of human skin cells grown in test tubes and again can produce results far superior to the testing of chemicals on an animal skin.

Microfluidic chips are being developed – these are lined with human cells and recreate the functions of human organs. Computer models like virtual reconstructions of human molecular structures can predict the toxicity of substances without the invasive experiments that are done on animals.

Animals actually make inferior test subjects because they are different from humans. I'll give you one example of this.

In the 1950s, the morning sickness pill thalidomide was tested on animals prior to commercial release with no adverse effects. Thalidomide caused over 24,000 babies to be born with severe deformities. Because of this they then tested again on pregnant mice, rats, guinea pigs, cats and hamsters and did not get any congenital disabilities unless the dose was administered at extremely high levels.

This is not a rare case – there are so many other examples some not too severe but others that have resulted in thousands of deaths before being pulled from the market.

And if you're just a pet lover, did you see the dogs in the previous image? Well, cats are used also used. Yes, testing can be done on any animal.

At the end of 2019, it came to my attention that the Lincoln University Animal Ethics Committee (in New Zealand) had approved two experiments. The objectives were to test the primary poisoning risk of sodium nitrite on native animals in one experiment, and the secondary poisoning risk on dogs, cats and chickens who might eat the poisoned carcasses in a related experiment.

Chickens, pigeons, mallard ducks and wetas (the weta is a native New Zealand large insect) were used in the first experiment.

They used a modification of the LD50 test - the lethal dose of a substance required to kill fifty per cent of the test animals. A cruel and outdated test developed in 1927!

Chickens and domestic mallard ducks were poisoned by force-feeding them; sticking a plastic tube deep into their throats and injecting the poison straight into their crops.

Shortly after, they were struggling to breathe, were vomiting, and had diarrhoea. They died painfully slow deaths with one duck in agony for forty-eight minutes before finally giving up and dying. The researcher watched on while the innocent animals died a horrible death.

In another part of the same experiment, ducks, chickens, pigeons, budgies and wetas were offered the poisonous food, but luckily not all animals ate the poison.

Sadly, not eating the food didn't mean they got off lightly.

After the feeding phase, the researchers killed most of the animals for dissection. The wetas were killed by freezing them and then grinding them into a paste with mortar and pestle. I'm not sure what the purpose of the paste was.

The other experiment consisted of testing the secondary poisoning risk of the test substance on animals (dogs, cats and chickens) eating poisoned carcasses.

Ten various breeds of dogs from the pound were transported to the test facility. These dogs were fed poisoned possum for several days on end.
A researcher watched for the dogs to display signs of poisoning (vomiting, excessive thirst, diarrhoea, heavy panting, fainting, and bluish colouring of lips, gums, paws and nose), but luckily none of the dogs showed any apparent signs.

Again, surviving the poisoning did not help their fate. Like the other animals, all dogs were killed after the experiment.

Ten cats were caught from the wild. They fed them poisoned possum for several days, after which the cats, too, were killed. Ten chickens were bought from a commercial farm, fed poisoned possum and killed through gassing them with carbon dioxide.

These experiments are so unbelievably cruel on so many levels.

Approximately 200 animals lost their lives all in the name of research.

Aside from the fact that vivisection is insanely cruel, there is no reason in this 21st century to be testing on animals.
Please support the companies that DON'T do animal testing.

I realise this has been a rather long chapter, but I want to make sure that you understand why vegans are so committed to helping stop the cruel, insane and utterly pointless use of animals when there is no need or purpose.

Both this chapter and the previous one is the fundamental principle for a person to adopt a vegan lifestyle. Going vegan is not about the food as the modern-day trend seems to imply but encompasses all animal exploitation.

However, with the increase in both the vegan and plant-based movements, it is nice to know that half a billion animals have been spared since 2007 to the end of 2018. I am sure this number will increase even though the meat industry will still survive for the foreseeable future.

Now grab your prayer wheel, shawl, beads or holy book and let's head to the next chapter to see where vegans stand within the religious context.

5 – The Religious View

Before I even begin this chapter, I want to make it clear that I am not a theologian, nor do I adhere to any particular religion. I do have a fascination to the different interpretations and the history surrounding man's interaction with his chosen God, however, this chapter is mainly concentrating on the Christian belief rather than going into depth with all religions.

Some religions have the fundamental belief one should not eat meat. I'm quite sure you believe Buddhists are vegetarians, but in reality, not all followers in this or other religions adhere to the principle.
Jainism is the one where vegetarianism is mandatory. Buddhists and Hindus, which are the most likely to advocate vegetarianism, leave it up to the individual. Of course, many religions believe in reincarnation (such as Hinduism), and so their followers refrain from eating meat as they hold the belief they may come back as an animal.

Going into the early scriptures of Christianity (also appears in Judaism and Islam) the plant-based diet is the one that was instructed by God to Adam and Eve. Genesis 1:29-30

> *"Then God said, 'I give you every seed-bearing plant on the face of the whole earth and every tree that has fruit with seed in it. They will be yours for food."*

These early teachings favoured veganism as a way of life. Judaism, as with others, advocates treating the environment with respect.

Sadly, animal agriculture does the complete opposite by squandering water, energy, land, and other resources. Most of these religions hold that human life is sacred and that we should care for our health. This makes you wonder why, since it has been proven animal-based foods increases the risk of heart disease, diabetes, and certain cancers, that the religious leaders are not teaching their followers to move towards a plant-based diet.

The central core of all the gods' teachings of the different religions is love, compassion, and mercy. Can you see Jesus looking at the current factory farms and slaughterhouses and then sitting down to happily consume flesh?

Now I'm going to take teachings from the Christian bible (although many of the stories from the Old Testament appear in other holy books usually with slight variations).
We all know the story of Noah and that he took two of each animal onboard the ark. This made me wonder at the logic of God regarding which animals he allowed to be food and wouldn't that have meant extinction for those animals? But delve deeper, and you'll find that, in fact, God instructed Noah to take several pairs of certain animals and these were to be for food.

It did rain for forty days and forty nights but Noah and his family remained onboard for around a year. This gave plenty of time for the animals, designated as food, to procreate.

When the year was up, Noah left the ark. The flood had damaged the earth so much that time was needed to get the land back to fertility in order to grow plants to eating maturity. God sanctioned the continued eating of animal flesh for the family to survive.

By now, I can guarantee that they would have got the taste for flesh, something that is still very much in the psyche of meat-eaters today.

It is interesting that man became weaker after the flood, even the flora was of inferior quality in comparison to pre-flood time. God also decided that man was to have a shorter lifespan, and so according to Genesis 6:3, it was reduced to 120 years. Noah had lived till he was 950, so a drop of 830 years certainly was massive.
I do wonder if this reduction in life span was caused more because of the change in eating from pure plants to animal protein.

Within the teachings of Christianity, there is the principle that one should administer to the poor and the hungry. However, with the increase in meat consumption Christians are finding it hard to come to terms with the fact that meat-eating is an inefficient way to farm. This is due to a large proportion of the grains being fed to animals. In the USA alone, sixty-six per cent of the grains grown goes to the animals. This is a real waste of calories and proteins, not to mention the land that could be growing a wide variety of plants for humans. The rich minority of the world is devouring the meat taking an unfair advantage. Even within the developed countries, poverty and hunger are rife. Fast foods are cheap, but they don't give any sustenance, and so hunger is ever-present.

Of the eight main religions around the world, the one thing they have in common is compassion. In saying that, they all vary in their commitment and the way they express this particular virtue. As mentioned, the Eastern religions such as Jainism, Hinduism, and Buddhism do, on the whole, support a non-violent and meat-free diet. Western religions such as Christianity, Judaism and Islam don't seem to share the same ideas believing that animals are there to be eaten and turning a blind eye to their suffering. They will argue that it is written in their holy books that God gave man certain living creatures as food.[11]

Now let us get into the word 'dominion'.

"But God gave us dominion over the animals" is a statement I hear quite often.

The word does mean to have sovereignty or control over something, for example, a king has dominion over his kingdom - a wise king will rule with kindness and therefore be well-loved. However, a king who is not loved will rule by instilling fear and using force to get what he wants. There are plenty of examples of governments taking this route of fear and force!

In the bible, we are told to be stewards of the animals and care for them deeply. God forbade the beating or whipping of animals and expressly stated that man should rest his work animals for a full day, just as he rested himself. Again, something that does not happen in this modern world.

Man is incredibly discriminatory over which animals he loves and which he condemns to a life of servitude and ultimately death.

> "God gave us free will, which I will never understand as we do so much damage ... but then we are held to account over this too at the Last day. So it DOES matter[12] to God ultimately, and very deeply so. We have been given much responsibility. What an amazing

---

[11] Said slightly differently in each holy book, but the same meaning.

[12] Regarding the animals.

gift, to give fallen beings[13] so much freedom to choose
... even to their own detriment. Anything less would be
despotism."
– Caleb Day.

Now I want to mention the idea of animal sacrifice and the reasoning behind it (as I understand it).

Remember that humans were born with inherent sin and live their lives pretty much sinning on a regular basis (I'm referring to sins against God and other men).

So, God commanded animal sacrifice so that the individual could experience the pain and heartache God had every time man sinned against him. His reasoning was that man, having a love for the innocence of the animal, would not want to kill it or see it harmed. God also wanted to use the sacrifice as a substitute for the sinner, meaning the animal would die in place of the man. Still, it was a temporary measure which is why the sacrifices needed to be offered over and over. Sadly, it seems man didn't have the same love for the animals that God had and so, as time went on, the animal sacrifices meant less.

Because it seemed not to be doing the trick, God decided to sacrifice a part of himself in the form of Jesus Christ ... the ultimate sacrifice. Has it worked? I think not.

As for the idea that veganism is a cult, I really can't see how it can be. Although a cult can be something popular or fashionable among a particular group or section of society, I see the growth of veganism

---

[13] Man

as being a conscious choice of an ethical or moral decision by an individual rather than a trendy wagon to jump on.[14]

Even though God allowed the continuation of eating animals, it was for man's survival (in some countries this still applies). But I question the need for the extension of this holy directive especially when the variety of plants are so plentiful and we now have many studies and research proving that we can be much healthier on a whole food plant-based diet.

Man has acquired the taste for animal flesh and secretions of which he does not need so he should question which has more value – taste or life?[15]

To end this wee chapter, I'm going to quote one of the verses I came across that sums up the fact that plant-based is healthy

Daniel 1:8, 11–12, 15

> *But Daniel determined that he would not defile himself by eating the king's food or drinking his wine, so he asked the head of the palace staff to exempt him from the royal diet.*
>
> *9 The head of the palace staff, by God's grace, liked Daniel,*
>
> *10 but he warned him, "I'm afraid of what my master the king will do. He is the one who assigned this diet and if he sees that you are not as healthy as the rest, he'll have my head!"*

---

[14] Although each day, it seems another corporation is jumping on the plant food bandwagon for profit rather than for ethical reasons.

[15] His life as well as the life of the animal.

11 But Daniel appealed to a steward who had been assigned by the head of the palace staff to be in charge of Daniel, Hananiah, Mishael, and Azariah:

12 "Try us out for ten days on a simple diet of vegetables and water.

13 Then compare us with the young men who eat from the royal menu. Make your decision on the basis of what you see."

14 The steward agreed to do it and fed them vegetables and water for ten days.

15 At the end of the ten days they looked better and more robust than all the others who had been eating from the royal menu.

See, Daniel knew what was healthy; just a shame religious folks don't follow his diet.

And, speaking of health – the next chapter is going to cover that.

6 – The Healthy Vegan

I'm going to go out on a limb here and to say that, if you are currently a meat-eater, there's a real probability you believe you need to have meat and dairy in your diet to get vital nutrients. Where you've heard that from goes way back, and even though it may have been your parents who said it, it was already in your psyche. For most of us, when we were growing up, we were told meat and dairy are an integral part of what must be present in the meals to maintain a balanced diet. Perhaps not said it quite in those words, but close enough. This is very much the carnistic belief, which I've already talked about.

Before I get into the health aspect of veganism in the 21st century, I would like to give you a quick biology lesson. Much as meat-eating people wish to disagree, we are in fact anatomically herbivores. That does not mean to say we can't eat animal products. However, if we do, we run the risk of contracting diseases such as heart, cancer and diabetes – more about this later.

With the anatomy let's look at the differences.
The main one is our intestine. An average human adult has an intestinal tract twenty-two feet long. If you measure the chest size of an adult, it is about twenty-six inches making a ratio between chest and intestine at 10.15. Herbivores are known to have an intestinal tract of ten to twelve times their chest length. Meat-eating animals have a much shorter intestine. Meat actual starts to rot as it goes through the gut and heads to the colon. Therefore, the shorter intestine means the rotting meat is not languishing in the system, but

the animal quickly gets the nutrients it needs and pushes it out of the body. Because of the length of the human's intestine, the meat has further to travel. This means that the rotting process increases ramping up our risk of colon cancer.

Longer intestines in herbivores allow time for the body to break down the fibre (only found in plants) and to absorb the nutrients.

You also need to know that not many parasites or harmful bacteria grow on plants, so herbivores do not need an extremely low stomach pH. Our stomach pH tends to be more alkaline than ones belonging to carnivores.

We have teeth designed to chew food rather than to rip and tear. They are broad, short, blunt, flat, and spade-shaped like the teeth of other herbivores. We also have the wisdom teeth that are really for helping us chew hard-to-digest foods such as roots, tubers, and foliage. In saying that, we seem to be evolving with slightly smaller mouths, and the wisdom teeth are either not there or are removed. I'm wondering if that is because we are now preparing our plant foods in such a way as to make them softer and easier to chew. Before you tell me that gorillas and other primates have large incisors, I'd like to suggest that these are used for the purpose of fending off rivals - a show of strength. Besides the gorilla (the largest primate) is totally vegan.

Staying in the mouth, we also secrete an enzyme called Amylase, which pre-digests carbohydrates.

When you compare us to omnivores – a true omnivore has a digestive tract that is similar to a carnivore, meaning it's short and highly acidic. They do have flat molars, as do humans, in order to chew the plants, but they also have larger canine teeth for tearing.

We do not have the necessary gut flora to properly digest meat as was concluded by researchers from Harvard University. In their studies, they put two groups on a five-day trial. One group could only eat meat and dairy for all three meals while the second group was restricted to a herbivorous diet which included vegetable, tubers, legumes and fruit. Their findings were dramatic for just a five-day test. The meat group had a massive outbreak of the bacteria Bilophila as recorded in their published report:

> "*increases in the abundance and activity of Bilophila wadsworthia on the animal-based diet support a link between dietary fat, bile acids, and the outgrowth of microorganisms capable of triggering inflammatory bowel disease.*"

It appeared the entire intestine was filled with these bacteria within just a day or two.

Yes, specific populations need to have meat in order to survive as where they live, they are unable to grow plant foods (or at least for most of the year). Mongolia is one such country, and another group of people who are often put forward are those who live in Alaska. The people of the different tribes around Alaska eat meat at every meal and scientists long marvelled at how healthy and happy they looked.

But look beneath the exterior, and you'll find a different conclusion. The life span is twenty years shorter than those who have access to plant foods. They suffer from many ailments common to heavy meat-eaters, such as atherosclerosis, a condition in which the arteries harden due to the deposition of fat and plaque on the walls of the arteries. Then there is the fact that twelve per cent of the population suffers from internal parasites due to the consumption of meat both cooked and raw.

There is another argument often put forward by the omnivores, and that is the fact that we need Vitamin B12. Absolutely we do, in fact, all animals need it. Please understand that NO animal (including human) can make their own B12. They must get it from outside their body in the form of a bacteria. Most animals[16] will lick bacteria-rich soils, and, indeed, humans can cultivate their own plant foods in rich soil that is free of chemicals and get the same result. If we did that, we would be able to assimilate our own B12 just like other animals. The trick is not to wash and scrub the vegetables as vigorously as we do, especially with chlorinated water!

One last point I want to make before leaving the biology lesson. We definitely are not carnivores as all genuine carnivores, and even omnivores eat an animal's eyes, nose, face, toes, tail, anus, inner organs, blood, brain, skin and fur UNCOOKED. It is interesting to note that humans are the only animal to cook food and that humans must cook animal foods[17] for it to be safe to consume – plant foods do not have to be cooked.

You've now passed the biology lesson, let's continue on with history.

---

[16] Most factory farmed and zoo animals are given B12 supplements.
[17] Even the 'raw' dish steak tartare has some form of acid or fermented accompaniment which will 'cook' it. Fish in sushi can be genuinely raw, but all uncooked fresh fish pose the risk of carrying a number of microbes and parasites that can cause food poisoning or infection.

So where has the notion we need meat come from? Most people have believed that we have always eaten meat right back to cave-man days. Palaeontologists have discovered that actually, we lived on a diet of grains, fruits and berries rather than meat. Yes, meat was eaten, but very rarely. Many also believe that eating meat is what helped our brains to grow (mentally). Again, this has been seriously questioned. The theory is that it wasn't the actual eating of the meat, but was the tribal life, the coming together and working as a team to hunt that developed the brain. We have now discovered that Orcas, who have never 'met' before, demonstrate a collective communication of hunting in order to be more successful when they gather for the massive sardine run. It appears to be only a few Orcas who have developed this skill and yet all eat the same foods, so if food is the driving force for brain development, why haven't all Orcas achieved the advanced collective communication? (Perhaps there are more who have, and we just haven't seen it).

Later on in history during the ancient times, we know that the Greek soldiers and athletes were plant-based. This was for stamina, endurance and recovery time as many of our current athletic champions are proving. Also, the Roman Gladiators, who were known as 'Barley Men' lived on a high grain plant diet.

The father of medicine, the Greek Philosophy, Hippocrates, is famous for this quote:

> *"Let food be thy medicine and medicine be thy food."*
> *- Hippocrates*

Not only did he believe in the correct food, which was plant-based, he also understood that good health was achieved with mind and heart as well. Compassion was an integral part of health and was just one reason he didn't believe in harming animals.

Did I mention Hippocrates was vegan? He was and this, for me, is one of the biggest ironies of modern medicine. Medical doctors take the Hippocratic Oath as they leave their studies. The modern oath really has very little resemblance to the ancient Greek one. Quite honestly, as the modern physician has no idea at all about the power of plant foods, the oath should be given a different name – perhaps it should be called The Pharma Oath as a pledge to uphold the practice of pharmaceutical medicine???

The whole concept of man needing animal protein to survive comes come from animal agriculture and dates back to even before the advent of factory farming.

Let's fast-forward to the 1950s when the animal agriculture industry became a real business. There was nothing to do with health in the expansion of this business. Any 'alternative medicine' such as massage, herbalism, naturopathy etc. which had been the norm, was now touted as quackery. The pharmaceutical industry also pushed the animal eating business as they could see a growth in modern diseases, heart/diabetes/cancer and of course, this filled their pockets.

So, from the 1950s to present day the marketing campaigns put out by the powerful animal industry just continued to increase as we saw the growth of radio, television and the Internet.

Back in 1992 the "Beef, it's what's for dinner" campaign started an intensive push for you to purchase beef. This slogan has changed over the years - "Beef. It's what you want", to the present "Discover the Power of Protein in the Land of Lean Beef" and even teaming up with the Dairy industry in 1993 to create the "Double Cheese Cheeseburger Days" campaign.

Beef is not the only meat to have hard-hitting campaigns. In 1987 the pork industry came out with an aggressive drive for their product starting with "The Other White Meat". This was simply to get consumers buying more by saying in their advertising that pork is as tasty, nutritious and versatile as any other meat.

Chicken used to be a real luxury; in fact, when I was growing up, we only had chicken twice a year – Easter and Christmas. Then around the 1980s, it became a popular idea that chicken was healthier than red meat.
Back in the 1950s, it took up to four months for a chicken to get plump enough for the table, hence the reason it was expensive and regarded as a delicacy.

However, since the introduction of factory farming, chickens are churned out at such a rate it has fast become the most popular meat. Healthy? Put it this way, the chicken of today has been specifically genetically engineered to go from hatching to dispatching in 35-39 days. My personal opinion is: *that is just not normal!*

In the late 1980s, we had just one brand of factory farmed chicken here that supplied the market. It could only be purchased whole and frozen. I remember going into the supermarket and looking in the freezer to get one when I spied, what I believed to be a turkey. When I pulled it out, I saw it was labelled as a size 20 chicken. Having grown up with backyard hens, I was stunned at the size and realised that something was very wrong. Needless to say, I put it back.

I do hear many people say that they don't eat red meat. Instead, they eat chicken, believing it to be the healthy meat. There is much research on chicken meat, and it all points to the chicken being the un-healthiest of the animal proteins! Chicken contains 266 per cent more fat now than it did forty years ago. That means there is 33 per cent less protein in the chicken, and it's all down to our modern-day farming methods. I have to admit it always makes me laugh when people take the skin off and maintain it's because that's where the fat is.

Poultry is the most common cause of serious food-poisoning outbreaks, and oddly enough you don't have to digest it to suffer. Raw chicken is so tainted that just handling it can cause a dose of sickness from mild to severe. Research from the UK, the USA and Ireland found that 41–84 per cent of raw chicken sold in supermarkets was contaminated with Campylobacter bacteria and 4–5 per cent was contaminated with Salmonella

Chickens are also filled with antibiotics and even organic chicken, which is supposed to be antibiotic-free, is not. This is due to a loophole in the law saying the antibiotic-free status starts on day two of the chicken's life. That means on day one all chickens regardless if they are going to organic or factory farms are injected with antibiotics. Sadly, a study done in 2012 showed that, even if you only have organic chicken, you are still going to be susceptible to the multidrug-resistant E-coli that was identified in 2008.

Marketing campaigns are all about getting you, the consumer, to buy more. They are there to get you to believe that meat and dairy are healthy, that you should eat and drink it and that there is no other way to get your nutrition. The nutrients they tout are protein, calcium and Vitamin D. As an aside, dairy is fortified with Vitamin D and so are a lot of the plant milk alternatives.

Hopefully, you now understand that it has been more about the industries' need to make a profit and less about the industries' concern about your health. If you do, we can now look a bit more subjectively into meat and dairy.

I'm sure you have heard the expression many times, "You are what you eat." Have you ever really thought about what it means? And do you think about it when you're making food choices?

In some ways, we do become what we eat, literally. Have you ever seen an example of your blood plasma after eating a fast-food hamburger? Probably not. What should be a clear liquid becomes cloudy with the fat and cholesterol absorbed from eating a high-fat hamburger.

> *"Tell me what you eat and I will tell you what you are."*
> *– Jean Anthelme Brillat-Savarin*

And when you think about it, we also become what we don't eat. When we switch from eating meat to a plant-based diet, we can lose that excess fat, are less prone to many types of modern diseases, and our cholesterol can improve. With obesity on the rise not only in adults but children as well, conditions like heart disease and diabetes are becoming the norm. It's okay, just pop some pills, and the symptoms will get under control.

We are raising a generation who will very likely die before their parents.

Many who decide to go vegan reach for the foods that resemble what they have been used to, fake meats to replace their burgers, chicken nuggets or meat pies (there are many others on offer).

Actually, when you think about it, it does make you wonder just how 'healthy' their meat diet was regardless of the animal content if they would prefer to replace their food with fake stuff.

Now, I do believe there is a place for these types of foods to help people transition, and it is terrific to see the growth in plant-based foods. The early companies such as 'Impossible Burgers' and 'Beyond Meat' were the pre-cursors to many jumping on the bandwagon. By 2019 the number of fast-food outlets offering vegan versions of their burger type meals had grown with nearly all at least trying a vegan option. When Kentucky Fried Chicken offered a vegan version of the nuggets and wings in Atlanta, customers swarmed to get to try it. The queue was close to 200 people deep, and KFC quickly sold out. This was just one of many examples of a big food brand 'trying out' the vegan version.

Much as I want this plant-based food revolution to continue my thought is, if you're about to step on the vegan path, why not start with the healthy version first? You see, the make-believe versions are, in fact, processed food. Yes, they are plant-based and won't have quite the same level of carcinogenic compounds or cholesterol as the real thing, but they still pose a risk to a person's health if consumed regularly.

Let us now dissect (great pun there), why animal products are unhealthy. We've been brought up believing that we need red meat for iron and all meats for protein with dairy for calcium. Here in New Zealand, we even have Olympic athletes who advertise for our beef and lamb industry giving the message that if you eat meat, you too can be a strong athlete.

Just so you know, the following information is taken from independent research studies published in prestigious medical journals.

It has been commonly thought that insulin spikes occurred with carbs and, because meat has no carbs, it was assumed that it would not cause any insulin spiking.

However, meat was tested and the results showed that the insulin does indeed go up. This was then tested against other foods. These were a large apple with all its sugar, a cup of oatmeal packed with carbs, one and a half cups of white flour pasta, a big bun-less burger with no carbs at all and half a salmon filet. The answer was that the meat produced the largest (and quite substantial) insulin spike followed by the salmon. Subsequent data showed that pork and chicken also gave the same reading.

The protein in fat-rich foods can induce substantial insulin secretion. In fact, meat protein causes as much insulin release as pure sugar.

Vegans have significantly lower insulin levels. Those who eat meat have up to 50 per cent higher insulin levels, which can lead to Type 2 Diabetes. However, put someone on a strictly plant-based meal plan, be they man or woman, skinny or fat, old or young and you can significantly bring their insulin levels down within three weeks. And the tests showed that add egg whites back into the diet the insulin production can increase by 60 per cent within just four days.

In the past, research and studies used to focus on potential nutritional deficiencies in vegetarians and vegans. It failed to see that many countries around the world have had a plant-based diet for centuries with no ill effects on the citizens.

Now, however, research has turned to a more positive angle, and it is recognised that plant-based eating is certainly nutritionally sufficient and in fact, is a way to reduce many chronic illnesses.

In the July 2009 edition of the Journal of the American Dietetic Association was written:

> "...appropriately planned vegetarian diets, including total vegetarian or vegan diets, are healthful, nutritionally adequate, and may provide health benefits in the prevention and treatment of certain diseases..."

So, what sort of things may you expect?

Lowering your risk of heart disease is a biggy. The World Health Organization reports that heart disease is the number one cause of death in the world. (The report was dated 2011, but I'm picking with the continuing rise in fast foods, that it's still up there in the number one spot).

Now we used to think that heart disease and high blood pressure was the result of ageing and that nothing could be done about it other than surgery and medication. Cholesterol, another symptom of the ageing process, going up the older one gets.

These now are, of course, totally busted myths from the past as there are massive amounts of data proving that they are predominantly caused by what goes in the mouth.

However, some myths seem to persist, and the one on our number one killer, heart disease, seems to take the top prize. For example, there is the belief that major risk factors like cholesterol account for only a minority of risk for people with coronary heart or vascular disease. Doctors believe that these diseases can be blamed on hereditary genes and that there is not much that can be done about it. If you have ever had to fill in health forms then I'm sure there was the question 'does anyone in your family suffer from ....' and a list of modern diseases was there to tick off.

If you have a family history of high cholesterol or high blood pressure, then it's particularly incumbent on you to revise your eating habits. Yes, there is some connection to hereditary, but for the most part, what is hereditary is what is being eaten, and that's the cause of the diseases. Think about it. One tends to eat in the same style as one's parents. So, if the belief is carnism, the likelihood is that you too will be a carnist.

I totally accept that there are rare genetic defects that do increase the cholesterol no matter what you eat, but that only occurs in 1:200 or even can be as low as 1:500 people, so, if you have high cholesterol chances are it's what you're eating.

Studies, time and time again, have shown that the overall lifestyle is what it takes to be healthy. That includes not smoking, some form of exercising and eating a whole food plant-based diet and that will reduce, even reverse not only cardiovascular disease but other diseases such as Type 2 diabetes and cancer. Up to 80 per cent of strokes are avoidable with simple lifestyle changes.

But, why not just take the meds on offer?
Well, pharmaceutical drugs typically only reduce cardiovascular disease by 20 to 30 per cent, whereas a vegan eating style can reduce up to 90 per cent, and whole food plant-based eating can be 100 per cent. Plus, there is the downside of side effects to all pharmaceutical drugs.

But if you are currently on medication for any of the 'modern' diseases, please seek advice from your health professional before going off them. Many doctors won't know about whole plant food eating, so might I suggest you get them to watch the documentary Forks Over Knives if they resist your plant-based diet. Alternatively, maybe even shop around for a plant-based doctor, one who perhaps is already vegan or vegetarian and who will support your decision.

I would suggest you delve into this further if you are looking at veganism for a significant health shift in any of the diseases mentioned above.

There are other health benefits, too:

Less likely to be obese: Most people who opt for a vegan lifestyle, lose excess weight without even really trying. It's one of those wonderful 'side effects'.

<u>Improved digestion</u>: With eating a plant-based diet, the fibre is taken care of, again, without really even trying. This is going to mean a great improvement in the digestion and elimination process.

<u>Increased energy</u>: Because of the improved digestion, you will get an energy boost, this is due to the fact that the body doesn't have to take up valuable energy digesting animal protein.

<u>No antibiotics or hormones</u>: Unless you have absolutely known how the meat you have been eating was raised, chances are you have been ingesting antibiotics and/or hormones without even realising it. Did you know that more antibiotics go to animals than to humans? And we know how readily some doctors dish them out.

Even beef that is 'grass-fed' and 'grass-fed finished' is not necessarily out in a paddock. The chances are that the finishing will be done with dried grass pellets which will have a variety of goodies within them. Another loop-hole to be aware of.

<u>Chemical-free food</u>: This is under the condition that you will purchase spray and chemical-free whole foods, (go to farmers markets and ask if the food is spray-free). If you are eating meat, unless you know where your meat comes from – did you know that chemicals are used on animals during processing? Plus, the animal is very likely eating food that has been sprayed with toxic chemicals. You may also not be aware that chicken is washed in chlorine or other antimicrobial wash after slaughter to try and get rid of the harmful bacteria is has.

<u>Healthy skin</u>: You'll be surprised how your skin will take on a healthier glow as your diet includes plant foods that are rich in antioxidants and vitamins.

Alzheimer's disease is another area that is being studied in relation to food. It appears in early findings that people living with Alzheimer's disease have higher levels of copper in their blood and in the fluid that surrounds their brain, as well as inside their brain. So where does copper come from? Well, organ meats and shellfish are the richest food sources of copper but so are nuts, seeds, legumes and grains. BUT the one factor is that copper intake only seems to be a problem when eaten with saturated fat or trans-fat. There are no saturated fats in whole plants. Start processing plants, and you can come unstuck though, and a good example is coconut oil.

As Alzheimer's is such a scary disease for families, here is a link if you want to find out more on this research.

Type into your browser: www.feeoshea.com/alzheimers

So, where will this leave you if you choose a vegan whole food diet?

Well, I would say in a very good position as far as your health is concerned and, according to William Castelli, MD, director for the Framingham Heart Study, you're much more likely to live an extra three to six years longer than your meat-eating friends. That may not seem like much, but remember, most of your meat-eating peers will be on some pharmaceutical drugs, perhaps suffering from inflammation or heart disease, whereas you will keep your health intact.

In some countries, even Insurance companies know the health benefits of being vegan and offer reduced premiums on certain insurance packages.

This is not a nutrition guide; I already have one of those which you will find on www.feeoshea.com/author if you are at all concerned about the ins and outs of getting the right nutrients. I'll address the most common questions of protein and calcium in the chapter 'Answering The Questions' further on. For now, the last thing I'm going to add is that you don't need to take a plethora of supplements.

My thought is that the average, healthy person shouldn't need to have supplements if their diet is varied with nuts, whole grains, pulses, fruits and vegetables. However, on a vegan diet, it is strongly recommended that you do supplement with Vitamin B12 and I like to add it's advisable to take Vitamin D as well. This should apply to everyone, including meat-eaters. A new report issued by the International Osteoporosis Foundation (IOF) and published in the scientific journal Osteoporosis International, shows that populations across the globe are suffering from the impact of low levels of vitamin D.

The problem is widespread and, on the increase, with potentially severe repercussions for overall health and fracture rates.

If you want more, there is a list of documentaries and books that you can access with all the scientific studies showing the wonderful results whole food plant-based eating can do for your health, and I suggest you check them out in the Resource chapter.

We've looked at the animals and at our own health, so the next one in this trinity of reasons is the environment. So, let's march right along now to the next chapter.

7 – All About Our Planet

We all think that the 60s was about free love, hippies and flower power. True, these things were happening, but something else was also becoming increasingly convincing, and that was the warming effect of carbon dioxide gas.

Rogue scientists also had the audacity to point out that human activities generated atmospheric pollutions, and this could have cooling effects. But this wasn't new thinking. In 1938 Guy Callendar came to the conclusion that people were dumping enough carbon dioxide into the air, and this would raise the world's average temperature.

> *"As man is now changing the composition of the atmosphere at a rate which must be very exceptional on the geological time-scale, it is natural to seek for the probable effects of such a change."*
> *- Guy Callendar*

So, it's certainly not a new thought.

What has happened over the past few years is that more and more scientists are accepting that sea levels are rising, the climate is warming and that we don't have any more time left to 'discuss' or 'argue' about who is right and who is wrong. We are fast approaching the tipping point (scientists say 2025 is the cut-off) and there will be no coming back.

I think I can safely say that we're all concerned about the state of our environment. Unless of course, you're in the Climate Deniers club, climate change is genuine and very much an issue that needs to be dealt with … NOW. We're well past the time of thinking about putting initiatives into practise that may take 20 or 30 years before we see any results.

Yes, countries are trying, and some wonderful things are happening, such as laws for new buildings having to have 50 per cent of the roof area in either solar or living green space and a real increase in electric cars. Prototypes of new aviation are being developed, again using reusable energy. Finally, some countries are realising that plastic is playing havoc to our environment, not to mention sea life and so single-use plastic bags and straws are beginning to be banned.

By 2019 many cities and countries around the world were banning single-use plastic bags, some even added straws to that but San Francisco led the way. They implemented banning single-use food ware plastics, requiring compostable alternatives to plastic beverage mugs, cocktail sticks, plastic stirrers and toothpicks. By late 2019 they had banned the sale of plastic water bottles from all publicly owned buildings including their airport.

There are some top companies also looking at trying to 'green up' their businesses and many new ones starting up are doing so with a much less carbon footprint than in the past.

An amazing conservation initiative in India has seen a re-forestation program not only planting trees for nature and the wildlife but fruit trees for food and creating sustainable income for people. In 2017

India planted 660 million trees in just 12 hours in a record-breaking environmental drive.

But is it enough?

In 2018 at the COP24[18] conference that was held in Poland a 15-year-old Swedish girl, Greta Thunberg stood at the podium and delivered a speech that was a blistering attack of these men and women who hold power.

She told them:

> *"You say you love your children above all else and yet you are stealing their future in front of their very eyes. Until you start focusing on what needs to be done rather than what is politically possible, there is no hope."*

Greta was at COP24 representing Climate Justice Now, a global network of climate activist groups. She told the audience that they only talked about green, eternal economic growth, pointing out that those in power did not want to be unpopular. And that's the kicker.

Since these Environmental conferences have been held, the first being in 1995, there has been no real advancement at all. Countries are still refusing to see that we have reached a point where we must act now.

Greta went on to become the beacon for climate action in 2019. In August 2018 she started skipping school on a Friday to go and sit on the Swedish parliament steps with a sign saying 'School strike for climate'. After her speech at the COP24 tens of thousands of school

---

[18] United Nations Framework Convention on Climate Change

children around the world joined the movement, walking out of school to demand action be taken.

Then in August 2019, she made a remarkable trip across the Atlantic to attend a United Nations climate summit (COP25)[19]. She did so without leaving a carbon footprint as she was aboard the Malizia II which had its own solar panels and hydro-generators. You see, Greta walks the talk. She is vegan, as is her family, and she travels by electric car or public transport (train/bus) when she needs to.

One young girl has done more to mobilise people than many before her. Her message is always the same:

"Listen to the science."

Midway through this century, there will be more than nine billion people on the planet. Already we are using most of the arable land that exists and overfishing the oceans. Water, too, is becoming scarce in many places.

The services that humans depend upon like a supply of clean water, food production, and protection from diseases are all subjected to dangerous impacts.

We are fast approaching the tipping point, and some say as soon as 2030 the window of opportunity to act will start to close and will be shut altogether by 2040 even before we've reached that estimated nine billion humans on this planet.

---

[19] The COP25 where Greta was going to make her speech was to be held in Chile. Due to riots the Chilean government cancelled it. It was then changed to Madrid. Greta found her way back on a sailboat and was able to attend. However, the UN climate talks were deemed a failure as governments argued and dodged responsibility, and thus ending the negotiations in a deadlock.

I'm sure by now you have heard or read about the ice-caps melting at both the North and South Poles. Why is this a bad thing? Well, the ice caps act as reflectors, which mean that the sun's rays are reflected back from the earth keeping the planet at a cooler level. Now when the ice melts, it reveals the dark water underneath. The sun's rays get absorbed, triggering the warming of the oceans. The melted ice also means more water in the ocean and rising sea levels threaten landmasses.

While we're talking about the ice melting, there's one more thing I'd like you to be aware of. Where there are frozen areas, (permafrost), over vast tracts of land, such as in Siberia and the Polar regions, it is known that underneath are layers containing vast quantities of methane, a potent greenhouse gas with a warming effect many times that of carbon dioxide. Melting permafrost will release this gas into the environment with unpredictable consequences.

So why would going vegan help the environment?
Did you know that people in developing countries are starving partially because of our greed for meat, dairy and eggs? Land is being used to grow feed for these animals when we could be feeding nearly half the world's population instead.

Animal agriculture is responsible for more greenhouse gas emission than all the trains, planes, rockets, trucks, cars and boats combined. Globally, cows produce 150 billion gallons of methane every single day. There is an argument out there that because methane doesn't stay as long in the atmosphere as CO_2, it's not as harmful, but it is far more destructive to the climate because of how effectively it absorbs heat. In the first 20 years after its release, methane is 84 times more potent. The trouble is we keep producing it because of our pig-headiness about "our right to eat meat". Even if we did stop farming the cows, we'd still be stuck with two decades of methane in the atmosphere.

The intensive farming is also playing havoc with the ecosystems around the world, and we are losing species at a rate of 150-200 plant, insect, bird and mammal every 24 hours. This is nearly 1,000 times more than the natural rate. Many say that it is higher than anything seen since the dinosaurs. We are, indeed, even looking at the extinction of the human species if we don't do something pretty dramatic really soon.

We have the misguided belief that the rainforests around the world are being stripped and turned into unsustainable palm oil plantations. This is only correct in a small way in the rainforests of Borneo and Sumatra. What is not widely known is that 91 per cent of devastation to all rainforests is caused by animal agriculture. Every second of every day, one to two acres of rainforest is cleared for the sole purpose of either grazing livestock or growing food for them. The majority of deforestation happens in Latin America but also in tropical Asia and Africa.

Every year the Amazon rain forest clears land for animal agriculture, timber and mining. However, in 2019 the number of fires being lit intensified due to the newly elected right-wing president Jair Bolsonaro in Brazil. Bolsonaro had come into power, declaring that he would open up the Amazon for further development and remove any protected lands from the indigenous populations.
Emboldened by this, in 2019 there was a jump of around 80 per cent of fires lit which meant more than 74,000 fires raged across the

Amazon growing so intense that they sent smoke all the way to São Paulo, Brazil's largest city.

The slash and burn method (illegal in the dry season) is to clear new land, but fire is also used as a means of replenishing the soil and encourage the growth of pastures for cattle.

A massive political argument broke out between Bolsonaro and the French president Emmanuel Macron who, along with the G7 leaders, committed $20 million to help with putting out the fires in Brazil and Bolivia. Bolsonaro rejected the money declaring that Macron had a 'colonialist mentality'. And so, the Amazon kept burning.[20]

There is one last thing to understand about the Amazon rain forest. Fire is not a natural occurrence there as it is in places like Australia[21]. Therefore, the plants are unable to regenerate. Where fire is natural, this is nature's way of restoring the soil and stimulating new growth. What burns in the Amazon, remains dead unless humans are somehow able to replant.

I want you to try and wrap your head around the fact that we raise 70 BILLION farmed animals every year, and these animals have to be fed and watered. More than SIX MILLION are killed EVERY HOUR to feed the seemingly insatiable human appetite for meat. This industry is the leading cause of species extinction, ecosystems dying, land destruction, water pollution and ocean dead zones.

We also have to look at the water. The meat and dairy industry uses one-third of the planet's freshwater. Many cities experience drought conditions, and citizens are asked to 'save water' by reducing their

---

[20] The Amazon fires were an ongoing nightmare and were not resolved by the time this book went to publication.
[21] Australia has a bush fire season; however, in 2019, severe drought linked to climate change was blamed as the leading cause for the early start to the fire season.

time in the shower, not flushing the toilet each time, turning off taps and restricted hose use. But animal agriculture is allowed to continue using freshwater. For example, one dairy cow will drink on average 113.5 litres/30 gallons of water a day, not to mention the other water needs dairy has.

To give you another example, one hamburger uses approximately 3000 litres/660 gallons from start to finish. That's pretty much two months' worth of showering if Jo Citizen was allowed to have normal ones. But, hey, he can still get his hamburger!

While on the subject of water. As I'm sure you are well aware, animals must pee and pooh, and this has now become a massive problem. As intensive farming has accelerated and numbers of farmed animals increased, most production systems do not have the schemes in place to deal with the massive amounts of excrement that is produced on a daily basis. There is far too much manure to use as fertiliser, and so it gets stored in open ponds or pits. Bedding waste, antibiotic residues, cleaning solutions and other chemicals and even the occasional dead animal can end up in these lagoons. Most are not sealed, and so the untreated waste can seep into the groundwater.

Many times, untreated waste is applied to fields, and any runoff can end up in streams and rivers. Add to this, fertilisers that are sprayed onto land, and you've got an unbelievably toxic mix going into our water supplies. It's no wonder many streams and rivers are dying, as are the dead zones in our oceans.

So, let me give you some stats.

- 26 per cent of the world's ice-free land is used for livestock grazing, add to that another 33 per cent which is used for feed production.
- 40 per cent of the world's grain is being fed to livestock.
- 55 per cent of water is used in animal agriculture and only 5 per cent used in private homes.
- Meat, egg and dairy produces 65 per cent of the world's nitrous oxide emission.
- One calorie from animal protein requires eleven times as much fossil fuel as one calorie of plant protein.
- Animals raised for food create 40,370 kilos/89,000 pounds of excrement per SECOND!
- If you exchange eating meat for a vegan diet, you will reduce carbon dioxide emissions by 1.5 tons per year.

We need to stop the destruction and reduce carbon emissions and start using the land for either plant foods which will feed the world or return it to nature to allow the animals to retrieve their habitats. It has been scientifically proven that adopting a vegan diet will have transformative effects, including reducing greenhouse gas emission by an average of 6.6 billion metric tons, that is a 49 per cent reduction!

But which government is going to be radical enough to demand their population give up meat, dairy, eggs and fish?
No government will because they don't want to be unpopular plus the majority of those in power are carnists themselves and refuse to see the environmental benefit of veganism.
Then there is the misguided economic argument that governments put forward. These are pushed by the agriculture industries who are looking out for their shareholders. An excellent example of this is

New Zealand with its continued support of the dairy industry citing it as being the second biggest earner for the country.

However, when you take a look around, you see that the number of vegans has increased very dramatically. At the beginning of 2018, it was estimated that the rise in veganism in the USA was around 600 per cent over the previous three years. In the UK it was 350 per cent. The trend doesn't look like abating any time soon. With celebrities, athletes, large companies and countries, even China, all supporting the plant-based movement this trend will have far-reaching impacts on our environment, not to mention the animals.

Yes, we have other environmental issues that must also be dealt with, the biggest, in my opinion, being plastic, but with the adoption of a vegan diet and lifestyle, we will give mother earth a bit of breathing space to heal.

Remember I said earlier that 70 billion animals are raised annually for food? I want to add that that number is expected to go to 115 billion by 2050. Do you think this is sustainable? Do you honestly believe we have the land to grow the food needed for these animals? Many who go vegan for the environment do so to lessen the impact that the animal agriculture footprint has on this planet. However, I feel that not only is plant-based the best option; there is also a need to get back to permaculture, to organic, to developing ecosystems and to looking after mother earth.

I think now would be an excellent time to mention the wild animals and what the human footprint has done to them.

For centuries farmers have protected their livestock from wild predators. It still happens in many parts of the world as tribes herd their goats or cattle through territories where carnivores are. In the past, these farmers have not had to kill many predators. However, with the significant changes happening in weather patterns, droughts are being seen across Africa. By mid-November 2019, Zimbabwe was experiencing such a severe drought that hundreds of animals died including elephants and buffalo. Predators and scavengers thrived, creating an imbalance. The Hwange National Park planned the largest relocation of animals every recorded. They moved 600 elephants, two prides of lions, a pack of wild dogs, 50 buffalo, 40 giraffe and 2,000 impalas to three separate parks.

Of course, the severity of the drought also impacted on the human population as well. Hungry elephants were raiding settlements in search of food, posing a threat to the communities. The UN warned that more than five million rural Zimbabweans (nearly a third of the population) were at risk of food shortages before the next harvest in 2020.

In the factory farming style, the animal agricultural system means the wildlife pays a heavy toll. Swathes of forests are destroyed in order to graze cattle or to grow crops to feed the ever-increasing factory farms. In doing so, many animals go extinct or have to move to other places in search of food and secure habitats. On existing farmland, both predators and grazing native animals are killed in order to protect the meat production. Arizona completely wiped out the grey wolf from its ecosystem under the guise of 'predator control', and California did the same with their grizzly bears.

Climate change is having an enormous impact on animals such as the polar bear. Due to the melting ice and the warming of the Arctic, polar bears are finding it more difficult to find food, forcing them to come into areas inhabitant by humans. The warming can also collapse their dens and can leave them susceptible to diseases.

The oceans are also being polluted, not only with plastic which is having devastating results on sea life but with the overuse of chemicals, runoffs from animal agriculture and a warming climate causing algae bloom which lead to fish die-offs and coral destruction.

Our ecosystems both on land and in water, contribute to the survival of the planet. When these break down, it can have disastrous effects.

I'm going to leave this chapter with some more thoughtful insight. This time said by the very wise Sadhguru from India. In December 2018 he spoke at the Soft Power India Foundation in Delhi and part of what he said struck a chord with me.

> "*If we don't make a serious turn around in the human consciousness, we will see that 90 per cent of humanity will be on chemicals. Already to grow food we use chemicals, to purify water we use chemicals, our air is full of chemicals, water is full of chemicals, and everybody is on some kind of medication. Before a huge percentage of human beings become chemically controlled, we must turn human consciousness around. This is the responsibility of this generation. This is our time on the planet. What we are going to make out of it is our business. Let's make it happen.*"
>
> *- Sadhguru*

Now you have got this far, I am hoping that there is something that you've read that has got you really thinking about going vegan.

I want to take you through some of the nuances of being vegan in the 21st century so turn the page and head to the next chapter.

8 – The Modern Vegan

So just who is the modern vegan? Taken from slightly loose statistics from the USA and the UK, it seems that the average age of the new vegan is twenty-four. Apparently, new vegans in the USA are going vegan at a slightly younger age than elsewhere. It also seems that most new vegans are coming from both the Millennial and Z generations. That doesn't surprise me as they are the ones most affected by the climate crises. They also are a lot more aware of what is going on than those of older generations.

There are more young families embracing the plant-based movement and we are now seeing a generation of young children going to school with vegan lunches. By the end of 2019 more schools in the USA were offering plant-based meals, although a bill to allocate $3 million for vegan options was stalled in the California legislature. In Edinburgh, Scotland, all primary schools were to have vegan lunches supplies early 2020 following a meet-free Monday program. This was an initiative by Paul, Mary and Stella McCartney who work to help people cut back on their meat consumption.

As outlined in the first chapter, the definition of veganism is all about the animals, and those following this lifestyle are referred to as vegan. By the end of the first two decades of this century, the word vegan seemed to extend to all sorts of things relating to the food rather than the principle or true foundation of veganism.

Because of these nuances, there are people identifying themselves as:

- Ethical vegan: the truest form of vegan. Someone who has stopped the use of all animal products including buying into animal exploitation in the form of entertainment, experiment and fashion.

- Environmental vegan: one who identifies the impact animal agriculture has on the environment and this is the biggest motivator.

- Dietary vegan: people calling themselves dietary vegan should really be saying "I'm plant-based". However, this is still not a well-known description hence the tag of 'vegan'.

- Raw vegan: an ethical vegan who chooses a raw food diet.

- Plant-based vegan: usually meaning that the person has gone plant-based for health but then has discovered the ethical side.

Perhaps it is easier to type the word or say 'vegan' instead of 'plant-based', or maybe it is because most people know that vegans only eat plants, (although there are still many who think vegan and gluten-free are the same). Whatever the reason the word is associated more with food than anything else.

Let me give you a couple of examples.

- If you are currently eating plant-based, perhaps for health or environmental reasons, and you are going on a long flight. You would order the vegan food option.

- If you are in hospital, you could tell them you are vegan to get the plant-based meals. Many hospitals now cater for 100 per cent vegetarians and have that option, but you have to make sure it says, (or ask), that it is definitely 100 per cent.

There is a bit of a misnomer that there are five levels of vegan, level five being the ultimate. Instead, the Level 5 Vegan originated from the Simpsons when, in an episode with Paul McCartney, Lisa became a vegetarian. Paul asked her to remain vegetarian for the duration of the series. Lisa became the only eight-year-old to follow a vegetarian diet for more than twenty years.

The Level 5 Vegan happened several seasons later when this level was defined as someone who never eats anything that casts a shadow. It's a term that is now widely used as a tongue-in-cheek to the vegan who takes veganism to the impossible extreme and will not compromise (not taking medication, for example).

It is not possible in the current world to be a Level 5 Vegan

But what about the people who are vegan? Again, there are degrees of veganism. It seems that the new vegan isn't always knowledgeable with the intricacies of the lifestyle, which is fine. Older vegans just love that new people are seeing the atrocious things happening to animals and doing something about it.

Are there levels of vegan? Is it black and white, or are there grey areas? Of course, there are scenarios of animal exploitation and/or suffering in just about every supply chain and in pretty much every product that exists. So, vegans have to make choices on these nuances.

This even affects the food the vegan eats as every single piece of fruit or vegetable has a blood trail leading from the field to the plate. Even the ground itself is partly composed of decayed animal remains.

Most plants are grown with blood and bone or fish fertiliser. Alternatively, factory farms can supply manure to crop farmers.

Combine harvesters can kill little creatures and most cropping farms employ meat-eating workers. Then there is the issue of land cleared for orchards or crops and the displacement and killing of native wildlife.

Meat-eaters are quick to point out to vegans the animals killed during crop harvesting; therefore, vegans are hypocrites. Yes, vegans know all about crop deaths. However, the meat-eater surely must realise there are billions more killed for them as the animals are fed the majority of grains grown (causing crop deaths) as well as dying to provide the meat. Not to mention the clearing of the Amazon and other forests for agriculture where complete ecosystems and animals are going extinct.

In early 2019 a British show called QI created a bit of a storm when the host, Sandy Toksvig, told the panel that avocados were not vegan. The thought process behind this statement was that the bees used had to be trucked, sometimes thousands of miles/kilometres to the orchard and that is unnatural and harmful to the bees. This would be against the vegan belief.

From this came a plethora of comments telling vegans they couldn't be vegan because:

- You own a pair of leather shoes.
- You eat avocados.
- You have meat-eating pets.
- You drive, and there are animal products in your car.
- And the list went on

So very often, people want to catch the vegans out, and social media is always full of these types of comments.

Another compromise the vegan encounters is leather. As I mentioned before, some leather is entirely unavoidable as it is a material used in so many different ways and found across a range of items. If you buy an airline ticket chances are, you'll sit on some leather in the plane seat.

There are also the animal products the new vegan may not be aware of such as:

- Cysteine in bread.
- Gelatin products.
- Beer/wine.
- Beeswax/honey/propolis in beauty or health products.
- The glaze on candy = resinous glaze, shellac, natural glaze, pure food glaze all come from hardened resinous material secreted by the lac insect.
- And to round this off there is whey which many don't realise is dairy.

There are other times when a vegan may be at the mercy of others such as in a hotel and trusting that the porridge has been made with plant milk or in the work environment when s/he is asked to go and buy cow's milk for the work fridge.

Even going to the dentist can be fraught with non-vegan procedures. Grafting surgeries can use animal bone, and some areas are not cruelty-free. Some of the regulations can demand animal-tested products.

Whether it is fighting oral disease, infections, or just relieving pain, medication can be used. There is a high chance that these are tested on animals, and even the capsules can be made from gelatine. Sutures are usually made from porcine or bovine sources even though there are many different animal-free types available. During training, especially for dental surgery, pig jaws are commonly used rather than actual human models.

Obviously, all the above is also found in medical hospitals and surgeries around the world – the medical fraternity is certainly not a great place for vegans to be.

Ideally, the vegan should live in a solar-powered bubble made out of organic hemp and be totally self-sufficient, relying on wild bees to help propagate all their home-grown food needed to sustain their existence.

But that's not the real world.

In the real world, many large corporations are jumping on the 'vegan' wagon, and this in itself is a good thing. Traditional supermarkets, fast-food outlets, butchers and bakers are now able to offer vegan choices alongside their 'made with animal' products. All these plant-based alternatives are a great way for the meat-eater to transition to the plant alternative and, hopefully, onto a healthier plant-based diet.

And this brings up another nuance. Should businesses that offer predominantly animal based products put the word vegan on the plant-based ones? There are many examples of this mainly within smaller businesses such as cafés and restaurants. Some larger companies did begin doing this in the early 2000s but quickly changed to using words such as 'suitable for vegans', 'plant-based' or use the word 'free', for example, 'dairy-free'.

It is extremely likely that once someone embraces the plant-based foods, they are then open to learning about animal suffering and the environmental impact animal agriculture causes.

Veganism is growing, and change is coming whether we want it or not. As I've already said, it has been proven that when ten per cent of the population has an unshakable belief, it will be adopted by the majority of the society around it. And once the belief goes above the ten per cent, the belief is adopted as quickly as the fire that spread through the Amazon!

I believe that the word 'vegan' will always hold true for the ethical souls who take on this lifestyle for the animals. However, in the 21st century, other pressing issues need to be addressed and semantics of the meaning of a word, while we go through the transition, should be put to one side until the plant-based movement holds the majority. Perhaps a new term could come about. Just as 'vegan' is the first two and last two letters of the word 'vegetarian', maybe a word could be created from 'vegan' and 'plant-based such as 'vegant' or 'plagen' and be given to those making the change for the environment or health.

In saying that, I have yet to come across someone who has gone plant-based for health/environment, who then didn't learn about the animals. Hence the rise of the modern vegan is, perhaps, just coming from a different direction and vegans need to embrace it.

It's time now to answer some question, so go ahead and turn the page.

9 – Answering the Questions

Many people find it quite easy to go vegan, especially if they have watched a documentary such as 'Earthlings' or 'Dominion' which show animal abuse happening in the agriculture industry. Others perhaps watch a documentary or read a book on what the animal foods are doing to our bodies over time and want to invest in their own health. Then you have the ones who make the change slowly, usually beginning with vegetarianism or just reducing the amount of animal products they are consuming. Any one of the reasons are perfectly valid and to be commended.

There is a list of documentaries and books in the Resource chapter at the end, which I encourage you to explore.

However, let me point out that people only choose to 'see', 'hear', and 'feel' when they are ready. People can go all their lives in the stubborn belief that they must have meat to survive. They have been sucked into the world of marketing by the meat and dairy industries and have acquired the taste for animal flesh and secretions. They refuse to witness the healthy vegans who are dominating the sporting world or listening to the doctors who encourage plant-based eating. They choose to accept the skewed research done by industry-funded scientists rather than independent studies published in prestigious medical journals.

We can't really blame them; this belief system has been ingrained in humans for generations. It is the belief system that allows people to choose to eat one animal but not another. An interesting demonstration was done by PETA that succinctly proves this point. It was in connection with dairy milk.

A woman went into the street with a tray and a sign asking people to try a new dairy milk. Everyone who tried it had good things to say about it, such as:
"It's very smooth."
"It's almost like a milkshake."
"It's lovely and creamy."
"Just the right amount of sweetness."
and so on.
Then the woman quite casually said that it was dogs' milk.

The whole mood changed. Many of the people became abusive. Some spat out onto the pavement. Some just had a look of utter horror on their faces. Most could not believe that they had drunk dog's milk.

The point is, we are conditioned to think the cow's milk is perfectly fine and healthy. The same applies to sheep and goat's milk all marketed to the 'discerning buyer' as the next hip thing to get into. But take the milk or meat from an animal we have deemed to be a pet and look out.

In the West, there is an absolute outcry each year when The Yulin Dog Meat Festival happens in China. It goes on for around ten days, and it's estimated that 10,000–15,000 dogs are killed and consumed. There are online petitions, social media goes berserk, and the meat-eaters absolutely are appalled as they watch images of these dogs in cages on T.V. screens around the country while they chow down on their pork pie, beef hamburger or fried chicken wings.

However, in the USA for one day of the year, Thanksgiving, an estimated 48 MILLION turkeys are killed, and no one but the vegans bats an eye.

What I am saying is that it's not their (or yours if you're still buying into the Carnistic belief) fault. They just are not ready to have their eyes and heart open to the suffering. They are not ready to ditch the dairy so millions of baby calves can stop being taken from their mothers. They are not ready to stop eating their steak, their bacon or their chicken. They don't comprehend that they have to stop in order for the animals to be set free from the cages and windowless barns or crowded pens where they live in their own faeces, are fed antibiotics to curb disease or die on the floor because their legs have broken under their own weight and they can't get to the water.

People live in denial.

People have an inbuilt defence mechanism that shields them from the truth.

It is like young people who go out joyriding, driving their cars at full speed. It's not that they have a death wish – far from it. They have the "it won't happen to me" belief. The same mentality applies to those who smoke, "I won't get cancer, other people will, but I won't". Sugar is another food substance that most people know they shouldn't have, and yet they continue to eat sugary foods because they won't get Type 2 Diabetes - other people will.

It won't happen to me.
It doesn't apply to me.

Most people in this situation have, what they think, is a very valid reason why they do not even wish to give it a go.

As I've said before, there are different reasons why people choose a vegan life. It could be because of economics, health or even for religious reasons. But choosing a vegan lifestyle is generally motivated for the welfare of animals or the lack of sustainability of animal farming as we know it today.

The following questions are ones that I have been asked over the years. They are very common questions and/or statements that people make.

What I will do is give you the short answer (a) and follow it up with a longer version (b). The reason for this is that there will be many who will ask (or make a statement) but who don't really want to know. So I give them the short answer and change the subject. Otherwise, I can get dragged into an argument that is tiresome as the other person has no intention of changing his/her mind.
But there will be others who are genuinely curious and so it is for them that the longer version is appropriate.

I'm going to begin with the two most common questions and the most common statement.

1. Where do you get your protein?
This one you have to understand is because conventional thinking says that protein is obtained from meat, fish, eggs, milk and dairy products such as cheese. These do contain complete proteins and all the essential amino acids that are needed for the human body. However, the make-up of animal protein is not conducive to good

health, as I have already talked about. Now meat-eaters have a real fixation about protein, and that's because of massive marketing over many, many years by the agricultural industry. They also believe that you can't get the right sort of proteins from plant foods. In fact, many think there is NO protein at all in plant foods.

Protein really wasn't considered way back before meat became a priority food. It was the advent of factory farming that the industry decided to ramp up the 'health' benefits of eating meat. Even now, we still see advertising of prominent athletes who get paid big dollars to promote beef and lamb as a rich source of protein and iron to build muscle.

As I've already said in the 'health' chapter, scientific research shows that animal foods are detrimental to our health and that plant foods are a much better source of all the necessary nutrients.

So here are the answers to "Where do you get your protein?"

a. Food.

Many have pointed out to me that you need animal protein to live to which I reply that I've been eating just plants for nearly twenty years and I'm still not dead that I know of.

b. There is protein in all foods, both plants and animals. In fact, most people eating an animal rich diet will get too much protein, and this can cause all sorts of health issues. And here's a fun fact, there has never been anyone recorded anywhere in the world as being protein deficient – like … never. If the person states - but you don't get complete proteins from plants, I will say: There are plant foods that have the complete protein like quinoa, soybeans and basic rice and beans. I just need to put peanut butter on grain bread for complete protein. But did you know, that the body actually stores the part protein until the other parts come along, then it does the combining and uses it? Isn't that marvellous!

As I've already stated, meat-eaters can have too much protein, which in turn can lead to a variety of illnesses such as:

- Intestinal irritation, constipation/diarrhoea and/or excessive gas.
- Dehydration – it's advised to drink 2 litres (½ a gallon) of water to every 100 grams (3.5 ounces) of protein. With too much protein, we don't drink enough water.
- Fatigue
- Headaches
- Dizziness
- Heart palpitation. The American Heart Association does not recommend a high-protein, low-carbohydrate diet mainly because they contain high-fat foods.

So why do meat eaters have too much protein? It's because all food, including the plant-based foods, contain protein to some degree and meats are definitely rich in it. For a new vegan, sticking with having legumes[22] every day is generally the rule of thumb to satisfy the concern over the protein issue.

Just a heads up on this topic - you do not need to combine foods, that is a myth that was debunked by science years ago.

2. Where do you get your calcium?

This is the second curly question that I get asked and one that indeed prompted me to write my Nutrition book. Calcium is definitely

---

[22] Legumes = beans, peas, lentils, some nuts, some grains.

an essential nutrient that you must have to keep, not only the bones in good shape, but it is also used for your muscles, hormones, nerve functions, and to help form blood clots. Studies have found that excess of dietary animal protein in conjunction with calcium as found in dairy, is actually one of the main causes of the disease Osteoporosis. Now I'm not a scientist, I'm not a trained nutritionist but I do have the power of deduction, and when I learn that people who live in countries that have no, or very little, animal products, especially dairy, have no sign of osteoporosis and are able to live healthier lives than we do, my logical brain does have to wonder why.

Besides, dairy milk is breast milk for the animal's baby. Why, as adults, do we need breast milk and especially from another species?

And so, to the response.

a.   I get beautiful calcium from nuts and leafy greens along with many other foods.

b.   I'm easily getting superior calcium from lots of different plants including nuts, seeds and leafy greens. The other beauty of vegan eating is that I've increased my vitamin C levels which means much better absorption of the calcium. Funnily enough leafy greens and all other veggies come with their own pack of vitamin C, so I don't really have to think about it.

I actually had a doctor ask me this question and then promptly give me a list of our government's recommended source. The list was made up of dairy products with cashew nuts and leafy greens being the only non-dairy items way down on the list. That's because in New Zealand we have a huge dairy industry that has a lot of clout.

Needless to say, the doctor was pretty impressed when my blood work came back showing excellent calcium as well as:
"Better iron levels than a meat-eater." Ha - go figure!

The third most common one is this statement:

3. I'd go vegan, but it's too hard.
Again, all too common. It is interesting that since the turn of the century, we have seen such massive growth in plant foods as well as the acceptance of veganism on social media.

The responses I use are:
a. In other words, you don't want to step outside your comfort zone.
b. Like anything in life, learning something new can be strange at first, but it certainly doesn't take long to adjust. Besides you can start slowly with a couple of vegan meals a week until you get used to having chickpeas instead of chicken.

I want to add here another tactic I have when talking to people about that comfort zone they are in.
I will ask. Have you ever shifted to a new city and had to make new friends? Have you ever had to give a speech having never done any public speaking before? Have you ever been to a foreign country where you don't know the language? All these things are unfamiliar and can be a massive step out of the comfort zone.

Plant-based eating is exactly the same, but once a person grasps the fundamentals, it becomes familiar. I wrote my book 'What to Eat Instead of Meat' specifically for the person who is afraid to step outside their square. These are people who are wanting to eat more plant-based foods but don't know how to make the change.

So, I usually approach this by likening it to shifting to a new city, or even a new country. You get given the opportunity to further your career, to take on a job you have always wanted to do. Plus, the money is excellent, so what's stopping you? Ah, you'll be going somewhere you've never been before. You won't know anyone, and it's a rather scary thought that you'll be in a city on your own.

But you go anyway. You step up to the dream you've always had, you pack your bags, say goodbye to the life you've known and head off into the wide blue yonder.

The first few weeks are a bit daunting, finding somewhere to live, getting familiar with the new job and the work colleagues and exploring your surroundings. But soon it's not so bad, in fact, you're quite enjoying it. Now you can start to build your life, and the first thing to do is go online and see if there are groups you can join who enjoy similar hobbies to you.

When you go vegan, it's very similar. Perhaps your family and friends are not supporting you at all, and so you have to get creative. But the Internet is a wonderful place, and there you can go into sites like Meetup.com or Facebook groups and find other vegans nearby. Even if there isn't anything already active in your area, you can find a café which sells vegan food and put a sign up in the window for other vegans to meet there for coffee.

So now we get into the other questions and statements that crop up.

4. I'd go vegan but my husband/wife/children wouldn't and I don't want to cook separate meals.

I don't know how many times I've talked to people who say that they would genuinely like to be vegan, but the rest of the family want to keep eating meat. In my mind, this is such a lame excuse, especially if it comes from the main one doing the cooking.

a. Agree, it may not be easy, but if you absolutely want to save the animals, then you'll find a way.

b. Getting your partner on board can be tricky, but a really good idea is to watch a documentary (*note: I will put in the appropriate type, e.g., health, animals, environment*) together. I know from the experiences of other people in a similar situation that this works.

5. Animals are meant to be eaten.

I will sometimes bring in the religious view that I talked about in the chapter on religion, but it will depend on whom I am speaking to. I remember talking to a couple of door-knocking Jehovah Witness men and asking them why they weren't vegan. Yes, according to the Bible, after the flood Jehovah said that man could use animals as food. However, in this day and age, there is no need to kill animals. We live in a land with plenty of plant foods, and shouldn't we be showing compassion for the animals who are suffering in our food industry? I did add a few more things to the argument, but I know I got them thinking.

a. I am assuming you're referring to the Bible. I choose to follow a life of compassion.

b. Animals have hearts and brains as we do. They clearly show affection, joy, and fear. Animals have an inbuilt instinct for survival, they don't want to die, so in this abundant country we live in why should we take the life of an animal who clearly cannot defend itself?

6. Plants feel pain.

If livestock consumes more plants (crops) than humans, then 'plants feel pain' is actually an extremely good argument FOR veganism.

This particular excuse always amuses me and is totally illogical. So how scientific do you want to get? Plants do not have a central nervous system. However, a central nervous system is not necessarily a requirement for a being to react to the environment. Even single-cell organisms can do this on a limited basis.

So what is pain? In a nutshell, you feel pain when nociceptors are activated by various kinds of stimuli: thermal, mechanical, or chemical. This activation is transmitted to the brain via neurons. The brain then forms a representation of that activation and thus the pain is felt.

Plants do not have these mechanisms. A simple reaction to the environment, as present in some plants, is not the same as pain. If we assume for a moment that plants can feel pain, can they suffer? Even if plants can feel pain by some system that is unknown to us, it is still unlikely that they can suffer.

Suffering requires a lot of higher cognitive functions, like emotions and memory. All the animals we eat as food have these functions. Therefore, my answers are:

a. Please show me the scientific data that proves plants feel pain.
b. Plants don't have the cognitive functions to suffer and are therefore unlikely to feel pain. Plants do, however, react to environmental stimuli such as closing when touched or, more commonly, heat, cold, night, and day.

7. If everyone went vegan what would happen to all the animals?

Shall we start by saying everyone will not go vegan all at once?

This is the human race we're talking about – fickle, stubborn, greedy, and so many can't even be kind to other humans let alone animals.

As the poet John Lydgate (later said by President Lincoln) once said:

> *"You can please some of the people all of the time, you can please all of the people some of the time, but you can't please all of the people all of the time".*

So, what would happen? (I will summarise some of what I have written before in previous chapters.)

It is humans who breed animals into existence for the sole purpose of providing the market.

As the demand for meat diminishes, so will the production of the farmed animals.

Now let's remove the words "to all the animals" from the question and just ask – If everyone went vegan, what would happen?

The first thing would be a dramatic change, for the better, to our environment. You only need less than half an acre of land on a vegan diet versus two acres of land for a meat-eater (per year).

It takes around 9,500 litres (2,500 gallons) of water to produce 500 grams (one pound) of beef, but it takes only 95 litres (25 gallons) of water to produce 500 grams (one pound) of wheat.

A lot of the destruction of the rainforest would cease. Even in countries like the USA, Europe, Australia and New Zealand where there are beef and dairy industries, topsoil erosion is a real problem. Then you have the grain that is needed for the feedlots. Again, hundreds of acres of rainforest are destroyed to make way for grain planting.

Fertilizers used in feed crops produce potent greenhouse gases along with methane gas from cattle and farmers who burn fossil fuels for heating and cooling of the huge farm factory buildings.
All these things have a significant impact on our environment and are not sustainable.

The world going vegan would also reduce world hunger: big statement – absolute fact.
At the moment we do have enough food to go around. However, even though we produce enough to feed all seven billion people and more, those who do go hungry either do not have the land to grow food or money to buy it.

It is projected that by 2050 the world population will reach 9.6 billion people. This is now where we look at the logistics of how we use the land – it simply will not be viable to have a meat-driven population.

It takes up to nearly six kilos (thirteen pounds) of grain to produce 500 grams (one pound) of meat.
Six kilos of grain would feed a village instead of just one family.
At present, twenty-seven per cent of calories come from animal products, and 1.4 billion people are starving.
If people reduced those calories down to ten per cent, there would be no starving people at all.

This is because it takes about half a hectare (one acre) of land to raise cattle for nine kilos (twenty pounds) of meat. Use that same half a hectare, and you could grow over 165 kilos (365 pounds) of protein-rich soybeans and seventeen times more people could be saved from starvation.

Of the 145 million tonnes of grain and soy fed to livestock, only 21 million tonnes of meat and by-products are used. The waste is 124 million tonnes per year at a value of 20 billion US dollars. It has been calculated that this sum would feed, clothe, and house the world's entire population for one year.

We have to stop trying to change the eating habits of other countries – it's not going to do the world any favours.

There are still countries, especially in Asia, that are primarily vegetarian and India would probably be the number one vegetarian country in the world. However, with the western style of eating meat fast becoming popular, it means that the demand for meat is growing. China has seen a growth rate in its middle-class and subsequently a huge growth in Western foods. On the downside, there is a massive growth in the Western-style diseases. Heart disease, Type 2 diabetes, colon and other cancers, as well as osteoporosis, have all risen right alongside the animal foods that the middle-class and wealthy are consuming.

One last observation. In the current system, there is no money in the world of being healthy. The agriculture industry continues to belt out the scientifically debunked arguments that meat, dairy and eggs are healthy and should be included in the food pyramid.

My answers are:

a. Won't happen, the ag industry would lose too much money.

b.   There is no way that everyone will go vegan overnight, but the more that people adopt this lifestyle the less demand there will be, therefore fewer animals will be bred into existence, and slowly the factory farms will be phased out.

8. I don't want to be left out.

This statement comes in different guises, but they all refer to peer pressure. I want to expand on it as peer pressure can be a massive influence on how we act.

Strange as it may seem this is one excuse that I can relate to. However, it's not an excuse that I agree with, as there is no reason why you should be left out from anything. This is especially true now as veganism is one of the fastest-growing industries in the developed world and the choices of foods offered to us grow by the day.

Therefore, even though the excuse is not so bizarre, it certainly has no basis to sustain a good argument for not going vegan.

The only time that a person may feel left out is when it is associated with social dining. If this is the case, then it begs the question – How many times do you actually eat out at places that do not have a vegan option?

For argument's sake, let's assume a person's social life rules his/her dining existence, and we will go through some scenarios.

1.   **The BBQ.** Possibly the most difficult for new vegans to handle especially if they live in a robust meat-eating area, (parts of the USA, Australia and New Zealand spring to mind).

The BBQ is generally an event that the person is invited to; therefore, the host is known. The easiest thing to do is to get in touch with the host, explain the vegan angle and take along your protein part.

This is the time that the pre-made 'fake' meat sausages and patties really come in handy. It is far easier to get them at the supermarket than to try and make them yourself, plus the pre-made ones hold together better.

There is the issue of sharing the grill of the BBQ with the meat, meaning cross-contamination. To overcome this, you can pre-cook your sausages/patties at home, wrap them in aluminium foil and put that onto the grill to heat up.

There are usually plenty of salad dishes and bread served, and you can always ask your host not to add eggs or cheese to the salads. Of course, you can also contribute to the meal by bringing something extra, so I'm sure you certainly won't go hungry.

Other scenarios:

1. You are invited to a **friend's home** for dinner. This really is a no-brainer. The operative word here is 'friend'. You simply talk to your friend and if s/he is concerned about what to serve you, then offer to bring a vegan dish for everyone to share. Ask your friend, though, to not incorporate animal products (as with the BBQ) into some of the side dishes.

2. **Restaurants.** The 21st century is wonderful and modern in most parts of the world, so this should not be a problem at all. Most restaurants will offer a vegan option. However, there are still some who are behind the eight-ball and simply do not

understand that they are turning away business if they don't get with the times, as Chef Ramsay pointed out in a tweet to fellow chefs. You have the choice if you wish to dine at a restaurant or not. Steer clear of places that do not have a vegan option of at least two choices. What this tells me is that the chef is stuck in the past and probably not very good. Checking the menu online before going out makes it easier, or if you are strolling the eating district, most restaurants have their menu at the door so you can look before going in. If it's a work event or pre-arranged by friends and you have no choice of restaurant, then phone ahead of time and talk to them about the vegan options. You will find that most places are only too happy to cater for you.

3. **Cafés**. These are pretty much the same as the restaurants above. If it is the 'cabinet food' you are after for a quick lunch, some won't have anything at all, however, may offer more 'meal' type choices. You will soon get to know who provides the best vegan food.

The above are the only scenarios I can think where you may strike a glitch. I have been to restaurants in the past where there has been no vegan option or only one that I don't want, and I have asked the waitress if it is possible to mix ingredients from two or three different dishes.

There has never been an issue doing that, in fact, my plate ends up looking and tasting awesome and the meat-eaters at the table wished they had ordered what I'd got!

It's something that I continue to do as a vegan, and I still end up with delicious 'mixed meals'. I've also found that a great chef can get so creative and will enjoy the challenge.

Dealing with holidays is similar to any of the above. Probably the only place I totally lucked out was at a wedding where there was nothing at all that I could eat. I had a bit of an idea this could happen so pre-loaded before I went... food that is, not alcohol.

So, to answer the question.

a. Just ask.

b. This is where good communication with whoever is serving the food is a must, and if you don't ask, then you definitely can get left behind.

9. I know farmers who really love their animals.

Loving the farmed animals is one I hear a lot. Let's get real. Yes, a farmer looks after his stock. He calls in the vet if one is sick or needs help. He makes sure his animals have the right food, and he regularly inspects their wellbeing. However, what we forget is that the animal is a monetary unit. The animal is a commodity. Without the animal, the farmer would not make an income; therefore, it behoves him to 'love' his animals.

But what he doesn't do is treat them the same way as the family pet dog or cat.

- Does the farmer use anaesthetic when castrating or tail docking?
- Does the farmer take young calves way from their mothers within a period of a few hours?
- Does the farmer artificially inseminate his animals so he can produce more animals to replace the ones sent to slaughter?

- Does the farmer send his animals to slaughter as soon as the animal can't provide the maximum monetary return or has grown to the desired weight?

'The farmer loves his animals' is an oxymoron. The farmer does any or all of the above and more with the expressed intention of creating an income.

Love is an intense feeling of deep affection which cannot be given to farmed animals. Why? If the farmer became too attached to his animals, it would be too difficult to slaughter them or see them suffer.

Answers:

a. Do you love your dog or cat? Would you kill it to eat when there is plenty of other things to eat? – I rest my case.

b. Farmers do treat their animals well (generally speaking), but I question the word 'love' as the animal is a monetary unit and is sent to slaughter once it is no longer viable. Not like a pet that becomes part of the family and lives its life to the end. If we kill a family pet, we take it to the vet where it will be gently euthanized. We do not send it to a slaughterhouse to have its throat slit or sent to a gas-chamber to die a tortuous death.

10. I only eat organic, free-range and know the animal has had a good life and is killed humanely.

Answers:

a. No matter how well the animals are looked after they do not want to die, therefore there is no such thing as humane killing.

b. The word humane means 'having or showing compassion or benevolence'. How can you put that word next to the word kill? There is no such thing as humane killing. Animals do not want to die they instinctively want to survive and will fight for it. To be humane would be to show compassion and allow the animal to live, not kill it for the sake of a few minutes of tasting pleasure.

Now, for your amusement, let me add a few more wacky excuses or reasons people don't want to go vegan.

11. I'm into sport so need the animal protein.
So are:

Fiona Oakes - vegan all her adult life. Broke three marathon World Records in 2013 and is now the fastest female to run a marathon on all seven continents plus the North Pole

Joe Namath - the legendary quarterback is probably the most famous vegan football player. Inducted into the NFL Hall of Fame in 1985, he was also one of the best players of his time.

Martina Navratilova - the Czech-born legend is one of the greatest tennis players of the 20th century. She won eighteen Grand Slam singles titles and thirty-one doubles titles.
Wimbledon stars **Novak Djokovic, Venus and Serena Williams**, are also vegans.

Billie Jean King - a long-time vegan, along with winning twelve Grand Slam titles and sixteen doubles titles, she's famous for her Battle of the Sexes match, in which she defeated former men's Wimbledon champion Bobby Riggs.

Dave Scott - holds the record for most Iron Man World Championship victories ever.

Carl Lewis - wasn't always a vegan. But he eventually went onto a plant-based diet to prepare for the World Championships in 1991, where he says he ran the best meet of his life.

There are seriously so many athletes who are on a plant-based diet so, if you haven't seen it already, I suggest you watch the documentary The Game Changers. It highlights the benefit of a plant-based diet in sport.

12. We have canine teeth for eating meat.

Another false argument that people use is the classic canine teeth argument. "If we weren't meant to eat meat, why do I have these sharp, meat-eating teeth in my mouth?" What do gorillas and hippos have in common? They both have intimidating large canines that are sharp. Both happen to be herbivores. Why do herbivores have canine teeth? Scientists have noticed that gorillas and hippos do not use their canine teeth for food consumption, but rather for defensive tactics. When threatened by a predator, or another member of their own species, they will often display their sharp canines to intimidate the aggressor. If the fight escalates, they can use them to good advantage. Scientists theorize that early humans used their canines in the same way, but these teeth have become a vestigial body part now; we do not display our teeth as a sign of aggression or defence. Nor do we use them for ripping up meat as carnivores do.

13. Vegan involves weird fake meat.

I have honestly heard this statement as a reason why someone didn't want to try vegan food. I tried to point out to them that the food on their plate was ¾ vegan and only ¼ carnivore and that I seldom have any 'fake meat'.

Yes, there are some odd-ball fake meats out there, but there are far more healthy, nutritious recipes using whole plant ingredients and are just as quick to cook.

14. Animals aren't killed for milk.

True... the cow is not killed in order to get the milk. However, many people have no idea that a cow has to get pregnant to produce milk and that her calf, if male, will be killed at birth (or soon after) also, that the cow is sent to slaughter usually after four or five pregnancies.

15. Cavemen ate meat.

Meat was not their predominant food source. As mentioned before, palaeontologists have discovered that early man's diet was plant-based. We evolved fingers to pick berries, not claws to kill animals.

16. Lions kill animals.

I've never quite understood this one – there's no logic to it and just makes me laugh. I usually ask,

"Are you about to chase a gazelle, sink your teeth into it, rip it apart with your claws and eat it raw? I think I can safely say you'd rather get your food from the supermarket."

17. We are at the top of the food chain.

Say that to a hungry lion then get back to me.

18. It won't make a difference; I'm just one person.

Where you spend your dollar matters. The more people switch to a vegan lifestyle, the more the food industry will cater to this food choice and animal production will diminish.

This particular argument is now completely out-of-date as we are seeing the massive rise in the production of plant-based products.

19. I'd rather focus on people than animals.

I applaud you for this sentiment. However, there is no reason you can't do both. Veganism is simply a matter of choosing to eat plants rather than animals and not buy into any animal exploitation. You do not have to volunteer for anything. You do not have to donate money or time, and you certainly do not have to travel to foreign lands or war-torn countries in order to save another sentient being. You can begin by reaching for the lentils in the supermarket, rather than the chicken wings.

Some other silly things people say:

I have discovered the following snippets and thought they were quirky, stupid or illogical enough to add.

> *On the phone to my mother, and she listed restaurant options as "vegetarian, vegan, and **ordinary"***

> *Fish is good for you, we are supposed to eat fish, Jesus was a Fisherman in addition to being a Carpenter.*

> *"I don't know what I'm going to feed you!"*

> *Auntie: "I'm making turkey frame soup. You'll love it. It's full of vegetables."*
> *Me: " But it's made from turkey."*
> *Auntie: "No, it's not. I boil the bones and strain it. There's no turkey in it."*

Me: "But you're boiling its bones, and that's part of the turkey."
Auntie: "Boy, you are such a fanatic."
Me: "Yep. I reckon I am."

"You're really naive if you believe people are going to stop eating meat for moral reasons."

Overheard at a restaurant: The next table had people chowing down on chicken while having a discussion about how they would NEVER eat dog.

"Why do you eat yeast? Yeast is a living thing! What about bacteria? How can you eat anything with bacteria on, that's alive! How do you know they're not animals???"'

"We only need beef once a month to get the b12 and iron it contains, and some of the other aminos"

So, do you have an excuse?
Are you already vegan?
Are you considering going vegan?

Putting all the chapters into the mix, would you go vegan or plant-based (assuming you're an omnivore), and if so, what would drive you?

Economic?

A meat-based diet can be very expensive. Fresh produce bought in season can be very affordable and can be prepared (dried, canned, frozen) so that it can be enjoyed later in the season. Vegan pulses are also extremely cheap and go much further than the meat counterpart.

Ethical?

After reading the chapter on the treatment of farmed animals do you believe this is an ethical practice? Is it right that we take the life of another sentient being just to satisfy our taste buds? If you are still not sure I encourage you to watch documentaries such as Dominion or Earthlings or any others listed in the resource chapter and the end of this book.

Environmental?

There is ample evidence that a vegan lifestyle is more environmentally friendly. Large ranching operations cause topsoil erosion, coyotes and other natural predators are destroyed routinely to protect herds of cows, which are slaughtered anyway later on, and commercial fishing operations are damaging the ocean's ecosystems. Our environment is dying as a result.

Improve Your Health?

Eating a whole food plant-based diet has been shown to be a very healthy lifestyle. It helps fight heart disease, reduces cancer risks, lowers cholesterol, helps lower blood sugar and reverse the effects of diabetes, lowers the obesity risk, and reduces the risk of osteoporosis.

And remember: just because it's Christmas (or any other celebration time), it doesn't mean you can't enjoy many of the same wonderful holiday treats you've become accustomed to, as long as they are prepared with your vegan lifestyle in mind. Bread and cookies can be prepared with egg substitutes, whole grain flours and plant-based milks. There are numerous choices for vegetable dishes and salads that can be enjoyed by both vegans and non-vegans alike during the holiday!

Just before you dash off to check out your pantry and head to the grocery store for some vegan items, please take a look at the next chapter to give yourself encouragement as to the company you will be in.

10 – Vegans you may Know.

There are literally hundreds and hundreds of vegans and vegetarians dating right back to the ancient Greek poet and philosopher Empedocles and the founder of modern medicine, Hippocrates. There's Leonardo de Vinci the artist, the poet Lord Byron and the writer Leo Tolstoy.

And when we speak of the old vegetarians, it should be noted that they were 100% vegetarian, so in the group of plant-based eaters. As previously mentioned, veganism is a reasonably modern term.

There are actors, writers, athletes, tennis players and boxers. Politicians and world leaders, revolutionaries and civil rights leaders. They are everywhere, in all countries, in all professions, both past and present.

You can search the Internet for a much more extensive list.

But to pique your interest:

Rosanna Arquette	Cesar Chavez
Alec Baldwin	Julia "Butterfly" Hill
Kim Basinger	Andrew Bartlett, Australian
Mayim Bialik	Senator
Russell Brand	Coretta Scott King
Jessica Chastain	Martina Navratilova
Omar Epps	Tony LaRussa
Corey Feldman	Hank Aaron
Anne Hathaway	Jack LaLanne
Paris Hilton	Billie Jean King

Jared Leto

Hayley Mills

Mary Tyler Moore

Leonard Nimoy

Sandra Oh

Ariana Huffington

Dennis Kucinich

Rosa Parks

Upton Sinclair

Clive Barker

Deepak Chopra

Kafka

Louisa May Alcott

Mark Twain

William Blake

Voltaire

Leo Tolstoy

George Bernard Shaw

Percy Shelley

Steven Jobs

Dr Ruth Bates

Casey Kasem

Don Imus

Novak Djokovic

Joe Namath

Scott Jurek

Bryan Adams

Travis Barker

Michael Franti

Alanis Morrisette

Sinead O'Connor

Prince

Alice Walker

Allen Ginsberg

Chelsea Clinton

Jane Goodall

Uri Geller

John Mackey

Robin Quivers

Mr Rogers

Yoko Ono

Vincent Van Gogh

Sir Isaac Newton

Leonardo Da Vinci

Ralph Waldo Emerson

Pythagoras

Plato

Lewis Hamilton

So, as you can see, if you are vegan or a plant-based foodie, you are in incredible company!!!

By the end of 2019 veganism had become a lot more normal, although perhaps not fully accepted by some. Vegans are no longer looked on as 'dirty hippies' or 'weirdos'. It is a movement that is becoming extremely popular with the trendsetters, the movers and shakers, the influencers, the intellects, the professionals and people from all walks of life. It isn't hard to do … it just takes a few steps, and an incredible journey of discovery opens up in delicious tasting food, healthy living, animal welfare and the planet.

If you are not vegan, then turn the page to the next chapter to see how easy it is. If you are vegan, then please share these seven steps outlined.

11 – Seven Easy Steps To Get Started

Step One: Make the Decision.

It doesn't matter why you want to make the change to plant-based or a vegan lifestyle, but it does matter that you make the decision and commitment to begin.

Making that decision is going to be beneficial to your health, the welfare of animals and the health of planet earth.

I have already gone through the many different reasons for veganism in the preceding chapters, but if you still are not convinced, then please do your own research.

Briefly condensing these arguments:

1. Money.

For those who cook at home and are on a tight budget, once you realise that vegan food is much more cost-effective, then it is an easy decision. Many good cuts of meat are just too expensive to be having every day, and even the 'cheaper' cuts can't compete with both the nutritional and economical value plant foods offer.

The primary reason I started eating vegan foods was about money. To begin with, I was just having meat-free meals a couple of days a week and saved on the household budget quite a bit. Then I began to discover other reasons to be vegan, and so my journey really began.

Remember a tin of chickpeas or lentils can go a lot further than a cut of meat. Plus, you have the added bonus of the fibre it offers.

2. Health.

Summing up the chapter on health: Medical research shows that a diet rich in whole foods and raw foods and very little animal product is much better for the overall health of a person. Vegans who have a balanced diet, are far less likely to suffer from heart disease, high cholesterol, diabetes and other illnesses as well as being less likely to be overweight.

Of course, the health improvement only works if the diet uses whole-foods rather than processed 'fake meat' type meals, and it is well balanced with legumes (peas, beans, lentils), leafy green vegetables, other vegetables, whole grains, nuts and seeds, fruits, herbs and spices.

A whole food plant-based way of eating is the only known diet that will prevent and even reverse heart disease. Researchers have found that it improves cardiovascular conditions such as angina (chest pain) and atherosclerosis (build-up of plaque which narrows and blocks arteries). Even if you have already had a heart attack, a plant-based diet has been proven to reduce the risk of a second one.

To find out more, I suggest the book Prevent and Reverse Heart Disease by cardiac surgeon Dr Caldwell B. Esselstyn.

3. Animals.

The more people turn to a vegan lifestyle, the less demand there is on the need for animal flesh and products, (and this includes fish).

The inhumane way animals are farmed and slaughtered causes many to turn to veganism.

If you want to look further into this go online and type into Google 'image sow crate' or 'image battery hens' or 'image animal welfare'. But be prepared for some disturbing images.

4. Planet Earth.

Intensive farming is causing havoc with our planet in more ways than we can imagine, including the use of land, deforestation, water pollution, and air pollution.

> *"The standard diet of a person in the United States requires 4,200 gallons of water per day (for animals' drinking water, irrigation of crops, processing, washing, cooking, etc.). A person on a vegan diet requires only 300 gallons a day."*
> *— Richard H. Schwartz.*

Frightening facts and that is just the water.

Again, go online to easily find more on the benefits that a vegan lifestyle will have on our world, both with the land itself and how it helps to feed the hungry.

5. Spiritual.

Many religions adhere to a vegan lifestyle, and many others restrict what meats can be eaten.

Those who opt for plant-based eating, regardless of religion, are, in fact, compassionate people even if they don't know it.

"Nothing will benefit human health and increase the chances for survival of life on Earth as much as the evolution to a vegetarian[23] diet."
~ Albert Einstein

Step Two: Choose the Days

During World War I, the USA Food Administration urged families to reduce consumption of essential staples to aid the war effort. "Food Will Win the War," the government proclaimed, and "Meatless Monday" and "Wheatless Wednesday" were introduced to encourage Americans to do their part.

The campaign returned during World War II and beyond when Presidents Franklin D. Roosevelt and Harry S. Truman used rationing to help feed war-ravaged Europe. Surprisingly enough, the health of the people improved. It is recorded that in England, due to rationing of both meat and dairy along with more exercise due to rationing of petrol, the English had the best health than ever before or since.

The English were encouraged to use any spare land to grow vegetables. This tradition has continued to today, and spare land is now allotted to those who wish to have a veggie garden. These small areas are called 'allotments' and can even be big enough to provide for more than one family.

---

[23] 100% vegetarian

Nowadays, in a few western countries, neighbourhood gardens are being encouraged. These, like the allotments, are plots of government land that have been designated to be areas where the neighbours can create a community vegetable garden. This is a great idea and one that, hopefully, will continue to flourish.

Former ad man turned health advocate Sid Lerner, in association with the Johns Hopkins Bloomberg School of Public Health's Centre for a Liveable Future, revived Meatless Monday in 2003.

Reintroduced, as a public health awareness campaign, Meatless Monday addresses the prevalence of preventable illnesses associated with excessive meat consumption.

So, in this step, you need to decide which day or days you want to be meat[24] free. If you are serious, then make it more than one day a week as the more often you have a meat-free day, the more familiar you will become to vegan cooking.

Mark the days on a calendar and get prepared to follow through.

Step Three: Check Your Pantry.

Now is the time to see what items you have already in your pantry that are going to work with vegan cooking.
Coming up is a pantry list. Copy this out, if you can, and go through your pantry and fridge and tick off the ones you currently have. From this list you will be able to see what items you don't have so you can add them bit-by-bit over time to your pantry.

---

[24] Meat-free means to be free from all animal products, including dairy and eggs.

I have not added herbs and spices to this list. You probably already have your favourites, and these are just as perfect for vegan cooking as for meat meals.

As time goes on and you get more recipes, there is every likelihood that you will add other ingredients to this list. Feel free to make any changes to the list, so it becomes personalised to you and your family.

When you are going through your pantry, check the labels to see if there are animal-based products within the items.

Divide up your shelves. Ingredients with animal products and ingredients without. That way, you will be able to easily see what is vegan and what isn't. So on the days you do have meat use up the products on the 'animal shelf'.

This list is only meant as a guide – you certainly don't have to get all these items at once. In fact, it's a good idea to leave this list in the pantry then every time you go shopping you might like to add an item or two that you think will come in handy.

So, let's now check your pantry. Get your pen ... and away you go.

> *"Don't dwell on what you're giving up – embrace what*
> *you are about to discover"*
> *- Fee O'Shea*

PANTRY LIST

☐ Almond butter

☐ Almonds

☐ Almond milk

☐ Adzuki beans

☐ Balsamic vinegar

☐ Barley

☐ Black beans

☐ Brazil nuts

☐ Brown rice

☐ Buckwheat

☐ Bulgur wheat

☐ Cashews

☐ Coconut milk

☐ Corn tortillas

☐ Ezekiel bread (much healthier)

☐ Filtered water

☐ Flax seeds (aka Linseed you can get already ground)

☐ Frozen vegetables

☐Frozen berries

☐ Garbanzo beans also known as Chickpeas canned with no added sugar/little to no sodium

☐ Grapefruit juice (check the label)

☐ Green tea

☐ Herbs and spices – your choice

☐ Hummus

☐ Jasmine rice

☐ Kalamata olives

☐ Kefir water (fun to make your own)

☐ Ketchup, naturally sweetened

☐ Kidney beans canned with no added sugar/little to no sodium

☐ Lentils all types canned with no added sugar/little to no sodium

☐ Low sodium soy sauce (Tamari is best)

☐ Macadamia nuts

☐ Maple syrup

☐ Miso paste

☐ Mustard

☐ Navy beans added sugar/little to no sodium

☐ Nutritional yeast (this is a great 'cheese' flavour)

☐ Olives

☐ Pasta sauce – Marinara with no sugar added/low sodium

☐ Pecans

☐ Pine nuts

☐ Pinto beans canned with no added sugar/little to no sodium

☐ Pistachios

☐ Quinoa

☐ Raisins and other dried fruit with no added sugar

☐ Rice crackers

☐ Rice noodles

☐ Rye

☐ Salsa

☐ Salt – pure sea or Himalayan

☐ Seaweed

☐ Sesame seeds

☐ Spelt flour

☐ Split peas

☐ Sun-dried tomatoes

☐ Tofu

☐ Tomatoes diced canned, no added sugar/little or no sodium

☐ Tomato sauce, no added sugar/little or no sodium

☐ Unsweetened cocoa powder – Cacao powder is better

☐ Unsweetened fruit – canned with no added sugar/little to no sodium

☐ Vegetable stock – no sugar or dextrose added/no added sodium

☐ Walnuts

☐ White beans canned with no added sugar/little to no sodium

☐ Whole fruit jams (check the type of sugar used)

☐ Whole-grain cereals

☐ Whole-wheat flour

☐ Whole-wheat pasta – (no egg)

☐ Whole-wheat pitas or tortillas

☐ Old fashioned oatmeal

☐ Wild rice

Step Four: Shop for the Basics.

It's now time to go shopping. Before you get to the list on the next page, I just want to go over a few basic things.

Vegetables:

Whenever you can, try to choose organic, locally grown and in season. A great place to start is at a Farmers' market, just ask if the veggies are spray free as most farmers will not be certified organic but will practice organic farming.

Get a good variety of produce that you can both cook and have raw. Note here that most vegetables are better cooked (steamed is best) such as carrots which have a higher amount of beta carotene when cooked. Many others supply more antioxidants such as carotenoids and ferulic acid than they do raw. But raw is lovely, especially in the summer and in salads.

This is also a good time to try something new. Here you can ask the farmer the best way to cook or use the vegetable or fruit. I've discovered so many new flavours doing this.

Fruits:

Like vegetables, try to go organic or spray free, grown as close to home as possible and in season.

Nuts:

These are an important source of heart-healthy fats, protein, vitamins and minerals. Their mix of omega-3 fatty acids, protein, and fibre will help you feel full and suppress your appetite. You need to have your nuts raw and keep portions small. If you must, you can dry roast them. Store raw nuts in the fridge. A word of advice, don't take the nuts from the container in which you keep them, they are very more-ish and you can end up eating too many at one time which is not the best thing for your weight.

Beans and Lentils:

Canned beans/lentils/peas are fine and certainly a much easier way than having to cook them. Just make sure to read the label to see that they have no added sugar and little or no sodium (salt).

However, you can make your dollar go even further if you get these in a bulk store and cook and freeze batches. Lentils can be cooked at the time of the actual meal but all others will need to be soaked and cooked first.

You will use a lot of these (lentils and black beans are my staple), so make sure you have plenty in the pantry. Refried beans are excellent as the base for Mexican food, quick and easy too.

Quinoa/Rice/Pasta:

Having plenty of these ingredients in your pantry means you will always have a meal that is easy to put together. Quinoa should become a real staple for you as it is one of the most wonderful foods ... a 'super food'. It can be used hot and served like rice, or it can be the base of a salad heaped full of wonderful greens, olives, capsicums, beets etc and eaten cold.

When buying quinoa make sure it is Fair Trade.

Sauces, Herbs and Spices:

Although I did not add herbs and spices to the super list above, it's great if you can have good selection. Sauces like Tamari, Soy, Tomato, Balsamic etc are also a must. However, do make sure that you check the label and watch for added sugar and salt. This part I leave up to your taste, some like hot (chilli), some don't like hot at all. It is these condiments which makes vegan food so delicious.

Animal Ingredients You May Not Know:

Some ingredients to watch out for are:

Gelatin: This is made from the boiled bones, skins and tendons of animals.

Carmine: Also called cochineal or carminic acid. Unless it is stated as a vegan product, anything that has red food colouring is made from the cochineal beetle – so not vegan.

Casein: Dairy protein.

Glucose: (dextrose) Can come from animal tissues and fluids or fruit, so hard to know.

L. Cysteine: Sourced from feathers or human hair. Found in bread products.

Whey: Dairy by-product.

Lactic acid: Acid formed by bacteria on milk sugar called lactose.

Pepsin: Enzyme from pigs' stomachs.

Lecithin: Comes from animal tissues and egg yolks. Also, can come from plants so product must say vegan.

Beeswax: From bees.

Confectioner's Glaze: Also listed as resinous glaze, shellac, natural glaze, or pure food glaze. Comes from the lac insect

Isinglass: In Beer and Wine. This comes from fish bladders and is used as a clarifying agent.

Albumin: Egg protein.

Vitamin A (A1, retinol): This can come from egg yolks or fish liver oil so needs to say it is vegan.

Vitamin B12: Again, must say it is suitable for vegans

Vitamin D3: Comes from fish liver oils or lanolin. There is a synthetic vegan version.

Now days when we have usually got phones with us, it is much easier when you have the product in front of you to just go online to see if an ingredient is vegan.

The next thing to do under this step is to copy out the shopping list on the next page, tick off what you already have and go shopping.

Of course, you can add to this list, these are just the basic items.

MY SHOPPING LIST

☐ Vegetables and Fruit – assorted (include onions and garlic)

☐ Nuts – Cashews Almonds Walnuts Brasil Pistachios

☐ Lentils - canned

☐ Garbanzo (Chickpeas) – canned

☐ Refried beans - canned

☐ Chopped tomatoes – canned

☐ Quinoa

☐ Wild or brown Rice

☐ Pasta

☐ Corn tortillas

☐ Tamari sauce or Soy sauce

☐ Tomato sauce

☐ Condiments - Basil (have the herbs fresh if possible) Thyme Oregano Rosemary Spices

☐ Vegetable stock

☐ Onion powder

☐ Garlic powder

☐ Natural salt (either sea or Himalayan)

☐ Frozen vegetables

☐ Pastry – vegan

Step Five: Think about your Meals.

Now it is time to think about the meals you are going to have.
You should consider all the meals – breakfast, lunch and dinner as well as the snacks you might want.

It's quite possible that your breakfast is already vegan, so maybe take this time to look and see how healthy it is. Are there some changes you can make to give it more of the 'healthy' component? Such as making your own cereal instead of having store-bought. Perhaps you can try an 'overnight oats' breakfast, especially if you're going to be rushing the next morning.

Homemade muesli can be really delicious and cost-effective as you can purchase nuts, grains etc. in the bulk section of your supermarket, make up the recipe to your own taste, have nowhere near the amount of sugar or salt that is in the commercial cereals, and you do not need to have nearly as much in your bowl to satisfy the hunger.

What type of bread are you currently eating? If it is white bread, which is highly processed, think about changing to a wholemeal, whole-wheat type. It may not be viable to make your own, as you may not have the time, but if you do, then please consider doing it. In this modern-day bread makers really do make the whole process so easy. The downside is that you can find yourself eating too much as warm, freshly baked bread is incredibly tempting – so watch out for that trap!

A vegan kitchen isn't complete without a food processor and blender. Something I recommend you invest in if you don't already have one.

This machine produces awesome smoothies, which is a wonderfully healthy and delicious way to begin the day. It also will be constantly used for mixing up many other food gems. I would use mine just about every day.

Lunchtime can also be very easy for the vegan.
Whether you make your own lunch or purchase it, there are many different options you can have from simple sandwiches to salads in summer and soups in winter.

Dinner is usually the main meal of the day, so that's the one you will have to think about what you are going to serve.
The questions are:
• Are there other members in the household that you cook for?
• How do they feel about having vegan meals?
If they do insist on having meat, just go ahead and prepare the vegan meal. Then, depending on what it is, you can either cook a steak or sausages for them and pop it on their plate, or, in the case of a stew type, put some of your vegan stew into a small, separate pot and add some meat to their part.

However, if you are the cook, I'd tell them that if they want meat, they can cook it themselves. They may be surprised and enjoy the vegan meal! Of course, you could simply just not tell them and see if they guess that there's no meat.

I am well aware that there are a lot of people (especially men), who feel that they have to have meat every dinnertime. There are some who will not try anything new and others who will. You soon learn how to get around this, and it is one of the major reasons I advise people to take it slowly, a couple of days a week is plenty especially if you have avid meat-eaters in the family.

Now let's talk about the actual meal. When you first start out, it can be quite daunting trying to get the idea of vegan cooking.

To make it easier, in the beginning, think along the lines that you are cooking a meat meal. Now, take out the meat and replace it with something vegan.

Here's an example:

A piece of chicken, cooked carrots and beans served with a tossed salad.
All you have to do is replace the piece of chicken. You could have a stuffed baked potato, (adding lentils or beans into the stuffing).

Or you could have half an avocado filling up the hole where the stone was with hummus and pesto or anything else you fancy.

Another idea is to have veggie patties. These can be made in advance and frozen, which then makes them a brilliantly quick alternative.

Having dinner at the table does make it a whole lot easier. No doubt, at some stage, you have been to a buffet. This is where all the dishes are laid out; you take a plate and go along the table choosing from the different foods on offer. Obviously, you choose the ones that look the most appealing.
Well, your dining table can be just like the buffet. The difference is that everyone is sitting around the table. The similarity is that the

different dishes of food are there for everyone to help themselves to whatever they want.

The sky's the limit as to what dishes of foods you want to put out. From tomatoes mixed with vegan basil pesto, a dish of hummus (there are lots of different flavours you can add to hummus), to mixes of different types of salads – orzo salad, bean salad, green salad, quinoa salad etc. Then you can have hot dishes – patties, falafels, stuffed mushrooms or stuffed potatoes etc.

Alternatively, you could make a Shepherd's pie using lentils instead of meat and have different hot dishes of vegetables. Or, make little pastry[25] pies (made in muffin tins), and, again, serve with different vegetable dishes or salads.

The beauty of having separate dishes on the table is, not only do people have choices, but it can be a time when the family comes together and talks about the day. Of course, the T.V. and phones are turned off ... now, won't that make it interesting?

Once you get used to it, you will find that you will be planning the vegan meal without any problem at all.

If you are not the cook in the family, then you need to approach the vegan meal in a different way.

Hopefully, you have a good rapport with the cook. Cooks are important people!

---

[25] you can get vegan pastry it is made with margarine rather than butter

As I have already written in a previous chapter, talk to the cook and ask if it is possible to have one day of vegan food. If s/he is agreeable, then you don't have an issue.

However, if not, then suggest that you do the cooking for that day. Alternatively, you can offer to find recipes, which will go with the ingredients currently on hand.

You can offer to cook just your own meal, or you can ask that the vegetable part of the meal be put into a separate dish prior to any meat being added.

The point is that you communicate with the cook and come to an understanding of what is going to work for you and for the rest of the family.

Before we leave this step, there is something else I will discuss with you.

There are two main things that meat-eaters don't like about vegans. One is that vegans can sometimes get onto their hobbyhorse about animal welfare or health or the planet.

The second thing is that meat-eaters don't really like change and they can be a little fearful, that, heaven forbid, they actually might like the vegan food!!!!

If there are meat-eaters in the family where you live, please be respectful when you are talking about vegan issues and try not to get into a slanging match – easy to do, but chances are you will not change anyone's ideas if you get heated.

Remember the saying 'lead by example' it will go a long way to keeping harmony and peace. I have known many families who will dig their toes in when the vegan keeps hounding them. If you do want to help create a change, then join a group such as Anonymous for the Voiceless.

The next step is one that you may need a bit of time for as you can easily get carried away!

Step Six: Go Online.

You need to have a good source of recipes and inspiration. If you want recipes, then the Internet is the best vegan recipe book there is for someone who is starting out. All you have to do is type in what you are looking for:

For example, type into the Google search bar – 'vegan recipe lentils' – lots and lots of websites will come up, and you will get tons of ideas. All you need to do is change the word 'lentils' to whatever you have, such as 'chickpeas' or 'refried beans'. One thing, always make sure you use the word 'vegan' when you are searching in Google.

Not only is the Internet a great source of recipes, but it will also help you if you want to learn anything. Many times, someone will ask you a question that you don't know the answer to. All you need to say is that you will find out and let them know.

Or, they will try and argue about the benefits of meat. In this case, just nod, smile and say, "I'm still exploring the benefits of being vegan and have yet to make up my mind." That usually stops their nagging.

Then go and search on Google anything they may have raised that you're not sure about. Just type in the question like: 'where do vegans get their protein' or 'what is a vegan' etc.

Make Google your friend. The other great thing is that you can veganise your favourite meals just by putting the word 'vegan' in front of it.

If you are really serious or do want to learn more about the foods, then my book 'What to Eat instead of Meat' is one I recommend. If you want the whole-food plant-based version for your health, grab a copy of 'Eat Vegan for 7 Days'.

Both books you will find at www.feeoshea.com/author

Tip: Get a journal and write in all the recipes that you have tried and loved – that will save you having to try and find that wonderful recipe again. I have a rather large journal. It has all the recipes that I have tried and liked over the years.

One of the great benefits of this journal is that, because I am a rather adventurous cook, I tend to make recipes up. I will start with a basic base of something, then add lots of other ingredients to it – the trick is that I write it down on a piece of scrap paper while I'm preparing it, then, if it turns out to be worthy enough (in other words, delicious!), I write it into the journal. I have learned from experience that it's very difficult a month later to re-create a recipe I've made. Of course, there are other delicious delicacies that I have prized out of other people.

Occasionally I've been smart enough to take a photo, but not very often! It certainly makes the journal 'pretty'. The beauty of the journal is that I can record any changes made as alternatives at the bottom of the recipe.

Once you do get your head around the vegan option, please use the Internet, create a journal, and experiment.

Take, for example, a recipe of mine that I call 'Quick & Easy Pies'. These are mini pies that are simple and yet delicious and to start you off, brilliant to replace that piece of meat.

The basic parts of the pie are:

- Vegan Pastry
- 1 Chopped onion
- 1 can Kidney beans – drained and rinsed
- 2 tsp Tomato paste

Most homes will have these ingredients.

So, all you do is sauté the chopped onion until soft, add the kidney beans and tomato paste and mix together mashing up the kidney beans a bit.

You could quite easily leave it at that. However, it would be a bit bland, so this is where it now gets adventurous! You can add whatever you like to this base.

For example:

- Chopped bell pepper
- Chopped broccoli
- Chopped cauliflower
- Chopped carrots

Heavens, you can add a huge variety of vegetables, (chopped and cooked) that you have on hand. Then it's just a question of adding great flavour.

Maybe you could sauté some garlic with the onions.

You could take this down the curry path and make it spicy and hot with curry paste and chilli.

Or for a more Mediterranean taste with herbs like oregano, thyme, basil, rosemary and fennel or even ginger and cilantro.

You can add onion powder, garlic powder or even vegetable stock powder.

Once you have added the flavour to your base, put pastry into muffin tins, put in the mixture, cover with pastry, prick and brush with something to create a lovely crust, (I use soy milk) and bake in hot oven for 15 minutes, turning down to medium heat for another 15 minutes and, voila, you have awesome little mini pies.

Note: Time will depend on your oven, so watch the pies during that second half.

Vegan pastry = in New Zealand you can get Vegetarian pastry which is vegan.

You can record in your journal under the basic recipe the different alternatives you do and which ones are successful.

Step Seven: Begin.

There's really nothing more to add. You just have to take that leap of faith and know that you are going to create delicious, tasty, vegan meals with the bonus of them being healthy.

Let's see:

- You have chosen your days.
- You have been shopping.
- You have got your recipes from Google.

What are you waiting for?

Get into that kitchen, start cooking, relax and enjoy the ride.

Now head off to the next chapter for an example of what to eat.

12 – Ideas on What to Eat

We are brought up on meat ... all kinds of meat, from beef to chicken, from pork to fish we have basically four types of meat to choose from.

Of course, there are the hunters who add to their normal meat with game (hunted), from venison to wild boar, from duck to pheasant and tuna to swordfish. And so, it is very natural for you to believe that you will miss the bacon and the steaks, the hamburgers and the barbequed sausages, the fried chicken wings and roast lamb.

However, going vegan is a journey and, like all journeys, it has a starting point. The starting point on this journey is to have one or two days in the week that you go entirely animal-free. Yes, that's it, just one or two animal-free days. That includes all kinds of meat, poultry, fish, dairy and eggs.

What I want you to understand is that it's really just taking the unfamiliar and turning it into the familiar. For example: Perhaps you decided to reduce sugar and so you started by not having sugar in your tea or coffee. At first, it tasted awful, but you persevered because you knew it was going to be much better for you. Now, you wouldn't even contemplate having sugar in that cuppa, and if you did, it would taste horrid.

The same applies when changing from cow's milk to plant milk. At first, it can taste a little weird but persist, and it will become the absolute norm making you wonder how you ever managed to keep cow's milk down.

Did you know it only takes two weeks to get used to a new flavour? It is because our taste buds (cells) renew every two weeks.

So, do you think it will be hard to do? Not when it comes to the foods! There are just so many different foods, flavours, cooking styles and tastes that you'll never get bored and if you really don't like one thing, there is always something else you can choose. As I said above, probably about the only thing you'll need to get your taste buds familiar with is plant milk. But again, there are lots of different ones to choose from – soy, rice, almond, oat, the list goes on.

Here is one day, just one day that you could slot into your meat-eating life once a week.

Breakfast
(I've even given you an either/or, of course, you can have the lot if you wish.)

Either – start the day with a Smoothie.
Into a food processor or blender place:
- 1 banana chopped.
- About 3 cups of chopped fruit (any fruit that is available plus a handful of fresh or frozen berries),
- ¼ - ½ cup of oatmeal, (soak it for about 15 minutes in boiling water first to soften it)
- 2 Tblsp ground flaxseed.
- ¼ tsp turmeric + a quick grind of black pepper.
- About 2 1/2 cups of coconut or soy yoghurt (or about ½ that amount if just plain plant milk like almond or soy),

Combine until creamy, pour into glasses and serve.

To gain maximum benefit, prepare the fruit just before using.

Or – Muesli: You can either choose commercially made muesli or make it yourself beforehand. Making it yourself does give you total control over the ingredients.

note: check the label for animal-free ingredients and remember it will be full of sugar

Mix up:

- 1 ½ cups of rolled oats
- 3 Tblsp ground flax seeds
- 2 cups of mixed nuts and seeds of your choice.

Into a blender put:

- 1 cup fresh dates that have been soaked in boiling water about 15 mins, drained
- 1 ripe banana
- ½ tsp vanilla
- ½ tsp salt

Blend until creamy then mix through the oats.

Bake 30 – 40 minutes at 135°C/275°F stirring every five or so minutes.

Should be golden.

Serve with your choice of fresh fruits and dairy-free milk.

Lunch:

This is generally easy as it can be as simple as creating a sandwich filled with salad type vegetables or a nourishing bowl of last night's leftovers, grains like quinoa, avocado and or hummus. In the winter, you may consider making a vegetable soup.

Dinner:

Dinnertime is usually where meat-eaters get stuck. They think along the lines of what they should 'replace' the meat with. Sometimes, this is one way to think, but if you are serious about creating lovely meat-free meals, then decide that you will choose an ingredient or two and create a meal around that ingredient.

You can easily stuff some capsicums, (peppers) with a mix of mashed black beans and mashed pumpkin, put in your favourite spices and/or herbs and bake for around 30 minutes. In the summer, serve with a salad, in winter go with steamed or roasted vegetables. Another is to slice thick slices of cauliflower, season with Moroccan type spices and bake – delicious!

Don't get too hung up about the 'protein' part; there's protein in everything. Usually, with meat-eaters, it's the meat that is the star of the dish. Well for vegans it's the whole dish that is the star. Lots and lots of colour and textures are what makes a vegan meal stand out.

But if you're really stuck, pick a legume, for example, lentils. Now, go to your fridge and see what vegetables you have. Maybe you have a pumpkin. Head to the computer, type into Google: vegan lentils pumpkin. Make sure to add the word 'vegan' for completely animal-free. Take a look at the photo below – and this is only the first three there are literally pages and pages of recipes!

You can do this with any ingredient you have.

One last tip – enjoy it! Have fun experimenting! Try something new! Remember, being vegan is not just about the food; in fact, the food is only a small part of this compassionate lifestyle; however, it is the best place to start.

Modern veganism embraces the animals, the environment and health and each one benefits with the vegan choice.

13 – Conclusion

As I was writing this book, it seemed like every time I thought I had finished, something new happened that I felt was important enough to be included. Even as I was writing this last chapter, there were raging fires happening in California where homes were being lost, and millions faced power cuts.

The Governor declared a state of emergency. Climate change is all too real.

Then during the editing process, NSW, a large state in Australia, went up in flames. It began with around 151 bush fires which quickly got out of control due to the parched earth and tinder-dry bush. The number reduced to around 80 fires. However, these fires were made up from the originals blending together. Now the fire-fighters were battling mega-fires. The state issued a 'poor' air quality alert for Sydney as the fires raged. At the time of writing this conclusion, more than 2000 Koalas had perished. The Koala has now and been put onto the 'vulnerable to extinction' list. This is one step away from 'endangered' as these unprecedented bushfires continue to destroy millions of hectares of forest. The Australian government still refutes climate change and continues to support agriculture and coal.

The vegan trend seems to have taken hold. There is a rising number of products on offer as well as governments that are seriously looking to make changes to health and environmental policies. Because of this, we can be hopeful we will see more trees planted than cows born in the near future.

What we eat is a personal choice, and I respect that it is your choice to continue to be a meat-eater. I will ask that you to take a moment to think that perhaps the animal you choose to consume does not have a choice in the matter.

Thank you for reading this book, and I sincerely hope that maybe something in it has made you decide to delve deeper into plant-based eating and join the continuing rise of the modern vegan in this 21st century.

If you have a moment, I will be very grateful if you would leave an honest review on Amazon – go to www.feeoshea.com/author this is a direct link to my author page on Amazon and you will find my book there.

You can find a lot more information at my website:
www.goldcardvegan.com
And if you wish to contact me, you can do so through my Gold Card Vegan website.

Have good food and
Be compassionate to all animals, including humans

Fee xx

About the Author

Creator of the Gold Card Vegan resource website and author of books about veganism and healthy eating, animal advocate, Fee O'Shea is all about helping others step into a lifestyle of healthy plant-based foods and compassion for animals.

In the '90s, Fee switched to a vegetarian diet due to lack of funds. However, early into the 21st century, she had begun to learn about the welfare of farmed animals both overseas, and more importantly, within New Zealand. It was this knowledge of the farming industry that led her to adopt a vegan lifestyle.

At that time vegetarianism was being accepted and foods were available. However, vegans were regarded as hippies or fringe activists meaning food choices were extremely limited. Fee experimented with many different ingredients in order to create more tasty and appealing food, and it was around this time that she launched her first personal website which she currently still blogs on: www.feeoshea.com

She is a member of the N.Z. Vegan Society, has a column in the N.Z. Vegan magazine and you'll find her involved with SAFE, a New Zealand organization which campaigns to stop factory farming. Fee also enjoys being out on the street with Anonymous for The Voiceless, helping to educate others about animal welfare issues through the Cube of Truth. Her speaking engagements are usually concerned with the health benefits of adopting a plant-based, animal-free lifestyle or about the modern factory-farming methods.

She has a Vlog on YouTube and Blogs on both her websites. It's on these platforms that she takes great delight in having a bit of randomness within the kitchen, bringing the latest news or giving her opinion on animal welfare, environment and even short-sighted politicians.

Her website, www.goldcardvegan.com is a resource for people who are concerned about the environment, the animals and/or their health.
An ongoing labour of love, it provides support, encouragement, tools and resources to help going forward with a person's vegan or plant-based journey.

Fee has three children and six grandchildren. All her children have followed in her footsteps by being adventurous and creative cooks and are extremely conscious of animal welfare and planet earth.

Go to www.feeoshea.com/author to find other books written by this author.

Resources

ONLINE:

Beef
https://beefrunner.com/2012/10/09/ask-a-farmer-what-do-feedlot-cattle-eat/

Dairy
https://www.ciwf.org.uk/media/5235185/the-life-of-dairy-cows.pdf

https://www.ciwf.org.uk/media/5235182/Statistics-Dairy-cows.pdf

Pigs
http://www.fao.org/docrep/T0690E/t0690e06.htm

https://www.aussieabattoirs.com/facts/age-slaughtered

www.mpi.govt.nz

www. pork.org

Chickens
https://www.aspca.org/animal-cruelty/farm-animal-welfare/animals-factory-farms

https://www.farmsanctuary.org/learn/factory-farming/chickens-used-for-meat/

https://eggfarmers.org.nz/egg-farming-in-nz/farming-types/barn

https://safe.org.nz/layer-hen-facts

http://www2.sustainableeggcoalition.org/

Dairy
https:// www.ciwf.org.uk - statistics

https://albertamilk.com - ask a dairy farmer

https://www.ncbi.nlm.nih.gov - productivity

www.milkproduction.com - management

www.fonterra.com - N.Z. dairy

Fish

https://www.smithsonianmag.com/science-nature/fish-feel-pain-180967764/

https://link.springer.com/article/10.1007%2Fs10071-014-0761-0

Environment

https://foodrevolution.org/blog/vegan-statistics-global/

https://blog.pachamama.org/how-animal-agriculture-affects-our-planet

https://www.ncbi.nlm.nih.gov/pmc/articles/PMC2367646/
https://foodprint.org/issues/what-happens-to-animal-waste/?cid=906

http://humanefacts.org/infographic/

https://www.sciencedaily.com

https://biologydictionary.net/harmful-algal-bloom/

www.theguardian.com/environment/2012/apr/13/less-meat-prevent-climate-change

https://www.carbonbrief.org/cop25-key-outcomes-agreed-at-the-un-climate-talks-in-madrid

Health
https://nutritionfacts.org/video/paleo-diets-may-negate-benefits-of-exercise/

https://www.sciencedaily.com/releases/2009/06/090630143523.htm

https://www.ncbi.nlm.nih.gov/pubmed/6389060

https://hippocratesinst.org/first-look-veganism

https://vegsource.com/j-morris-hicks/einstein-hippocrates-thoreauthose-guys-had-it-right.html

https://www.health.harvard.edu/staying-healthy/can-gut-bacteria-improve-your-health

https://www.ncbi.nlm.nih.gov/pubmed/22475798

https://nutritionfacts.org/video/alzheimers-disease-copper-and-saturated-fat/

www.webmd.com/food-recipes/guide/vitamins-and-minerals-good-food-sources

www.vegansociety.com/lifestyle/nutrition/sources-of-nutrition.aspx

Other:

https://www.carnism.org/carnism

www.fb.org/index.php?action=about.history

https://www.forbes.com/sites/davidebanis/2018/12/31/everything-is-ready-to-make-2019-the-year-of-the-vegan-are-you/#1b816c8357df

https://www.theland.com.au/story/6291345/farmers-ditch-slaughter-for-public-image/

Ed Winters TedX: https://www.youtube.com/watch?v=byTxzzztRBU
                https://www.youtube.com/watch?v=nrVEYTSe-o8

https://www.forbes.com/sites/simonchandler/2019/11/29/virtual-reality-used-to-relax-cows-into-producing-more-milk/#7019ef7356b5

https://safe.org.nz/fur-farming

http://www.respectforanimals.org/fur-farming/

https://en.wikipedia.org/wiki/Fur_trade

https://www.lcanimal.org/index.php/campaigns/fur/fur-trade-facts

http://fortune.com/2017/06/14/india-cattle-leather-industry/

https://www.reuters.com/article/us-india-leather-exports/indias-crackdown-on-muslim-run-leather-units-dents-exports-hits-jobs-idUSKCN1C81MN

https://www.sciencelearn.org.nz/resources/816-new-zealand-sheep-farming-changing-influences

https://careertrend.com/info-8239121-materials-do-firefighters-wear.html

http://www.brendadavisrd.com/to-d-or-not-to-d/

http://www.waza.org/en/site/conservation/animal-welfare-1471340294

http://time.com/4364671/zoos-improve-lives-of-animals/

https://www.freedomforanimals.org.uk/blog/10-facts-about-zoos

https://www.scmp.com/magazines/post-magazine/long-reads/article/2149910/tiger-selfies-chinese-indian-tourists-lead-cruel

https://whalesanctuaryproject.org/

http://www.pages.drexel.edu/~soa29/

https://science.sciencemag.org/content/360/6393/1116

https://www.rtanz.co.nz/new-animal-welfare-regulations

https://metro.co.uk/2018/10/18/eating-avocados-doesnt-mean-youre-failingat-being-vegan-this-is-just-another-way-to-try-to-catch-us-out-8049510

https://www.rethinkx.com/food-and-agriculture#food-and-agriculture-download

https://www.export2asia.com/blog/lab-testing-requirements-exporting-china/

https://ethicalelephant.com/did-china-end-animal-testing-2019/

https://vegan.com

Religion
Religioushttp://www.pages.drexel.edu/~soa29/Religious%20Issues.htm

https://www.focusonthefamily.com/family-q-and-a/faith/vegans-vegetarians-and-the-bible

https://wol.jw.org/en/wol/d/r1/lp-e/101997568

http://www.nuffieldfoundation.org/practical-biology/plant-responses-stimuli

Bible References:

Genesis 7 and 8
Genesis 6:21
Exodus 23:12, 23:5
Isaiah 1:11, 32:20
Proverbs 12:10, 27:23, 31:8
Hebrews 7:72
1 Timothy 2:5
Malbim
R. Hirsch
Abarbanel

Books:

How Not To Die – Michael Greger M.D.

A Clean Eating Nutrition Guide – Fee O'Shea

What To Eat Instead of Meat – Fee O'Shea

The China Study - T. Colin Campbell PhD & Thomas M Campbell M.D.

The Sixth Extinction – Elizabeth Kolbert

Prevent and Reverse Heart Disease – Caldwell B. Esselstyn M.D.

www.ingramcontent.com/pod-product-compliance
Lightning Source LLC
Chambersburg PA
CBHW032349280326
41935CB00008B/504